PRAISE

"Having witnessed Rev. Dr. Paulsen's work over the years, I continue to be inspired by the depth and sincerity she brings to the New Thought tradition. "That's a Good Thought" is a steady companion for anyone seeking spiritual clarity, offering daily reflections that gently guide the reader back to their own wholeness. This is a book of real substance and heart."

— *REV. DR. ROBERT BRZEZINSKI - SPIRITUAL DIRECTOR NEW THOUGHT MEDIA NETWORK*

"Cynthia Paulsen has created a marvelous tool to help us remember who we are and how the world really works! This set of readings integrates the essence of all spiritual paths, and it may be used on a daily basis or, if preferred, dipped into for guidance at any moment. Whether you are newly on the path or have been studying and practicing for years, these reminders will make a difference."

— *REV. DR. RUTH L. MILLER, PROVOST, EMERSON THEOLOGICAL INSTITUTE*

THAT'S A GOOD THOUGHT

For those who believe peace is possible.
Let it begin with us.

That's a *Good Thought*

Daily Wisdom in an Uncertain World

CYNTHIA PAULSEN

THAT'S A GOOD THOUGHT

Copyright © 2026 Cynthia Paulsen

Edited by Melissa Paulsen

Publishing Services provided by Edits by Stacey LLC

Published by Liger Corporation

All rights reserved.

No part of this book may be used or reproduced in any manner whatsoever without written permission from the author except in the case of brief quotations embodied in critical articles or reviews. For avoidance of doubt, Author reserves the rights, and does not permit reproduction or use of this work in any manner for purposes of training artificial intelligence technologies to generate text, including without limitation, technologies that are capable of generating works in the same style or genre as the work, without Author's specific and express permission to do so.

This publication is meant as a source of valuable information for the reader; however, it is not meant as a substitute for direct expert assistance. If such a level of assistance is required, the services of a competent professional should be sought.

For permission requests, write the publisher at affirmgoodthings@gmail.com

Library of Congress Control Number: 2026902729
Paperback: 979-8-9895504-2-5
eBook: 979-8-9895504-3-2

FOREWORD

When someone asks you to write a foreword, it is usually because they trust you to introduce not only their work, but also their heart. And that is exactly what Rev. Dr. Cynthia Paulsen brings to these pages—her heart, her clarity, her humor, and her deep, grounded understanding of New Thought principles in real, everyday life.

I have known Cynthia as a friend and colleague, and one of the things I treasure most about her is her practicality. She has a gift for taking profound spiritual truths and distilling them into simple, accessible language—truths you can immediately use, reflect on, and live into. She never complicates what Spirit intends to be clear. She has a way of speaking directly to both the mind and the soul, often with a spark of humor that disarms resistance and opens the door to insight.

Cynthia brings great energy to everything she does, but it is never overwhelming; rather, it's the kind of energy that lifts you, reminds you, and helps you remember who you are. That same uplifting presence is woven throughout this book.

That's a Good Thought arrives at a time when so many feel worn down by the world—its noise, its conflict, its unpredictability. Cynthia understands this landscape well, not because she stands above it, but because she stands inside it with the rest of us. And from that human place, she offers something steady, hopeful, and deeply spiritual: a daily invitation to return to Truth, to peace, and to the inner wisdom we often forget we have.

What I love most about this book is its gentle practicality. These daily readings don't float above life; they meet life exactly where it is. Cynthia reminds us that spiritual awakening doesn't happen in moments of perfection—it happens in moments of honesty. It happens when we pause, breathe, and choose a thought that aligns us with possibility rather than fear. Each page is a small doorway back to spiritual center. Whether you are new to New Thought teachings or have walked this path for decades, you will find something here that encourages you, steadies you, or nudges you just enough to shift your day. In a world that often feels chaotic, these readings help us remember the deeper order, the deeper Love, and the deeper Truth at the heart of all things.

It is an honor to introduce this beautiful work. I know it will bless you. I know it will lift you. And I know—because I know Cynthia—that it was written with the sincere intention that you live each day with more awareness, more joy, and more open-hearted possibility.

May these pages become companions to you on the journey. May they remind you, again and again, that a good thought is never "just" a thought—it is a doorway to transformation.

Reverend Robin Haruna
Senior Minister, Unity of Bandon
Author, The Ten Commitments: Entering the Promised Land of Abundant Life
Co-author, Wake Up – Live the Life You Love in Spirit

INTRODUCTION

Some days it feels like the world is on fire. The headlines, the conflict, the uncertainty—it's enough to make anyone feel lost, scared, and overwhelmed. But what if there is another way to see it all? What if inner peace, joy, and divine connection are always available, no matter what is happening around us?

In the early days of my New Thought journey, I took a ten-week course called Foundations of The Science of Mind®: Basic Principles for Spiritual Living. One particular session was entirely dedicated to teaching the class how to write an Affirmative Prayer (also known as a Spiritual Mind Treatment). I learned something interesting that day: before you dive into the steps of Spiritual Mind Treatment—before you start affirming the Omnipresence of God and your oneness with It—you have to state your purpose. You state the condition you desire to change, and you declare what you expect to experience when the condition is transformed. That is where you begin.

This book of daily readings is not an Affirmative Prayer, but like every meaningful practice, it has purpose. Let's start there. The intended purpose of this book is to give you something good to think about every single day—something spiritually inspiring, comforting, and practical—spiritual tools you can apply to your own life—*a good thought that helps*—every day.

Why? Because let's be honest, some days, the world feels like a dumpster fire of one low consciousness disaster after another. A quick glance at the news, and you know what I mean. It looks like humanity is experiencing an epidemic of reduced spiritual awareness. Or is it? I wrote this book, and you are holding it in your hands. Things can't be all that bad. At the very least, the two of us are willing to learn, think, and grow through these trying times. That means there is still light. There is still hope.

If you are like me, you sometimes struggle to stay in alignment with your spiritual Truth while the world swirls with chaos. That's why we need reminders, prayer, mindfulness, and spiritual practice.

We need practical tips and tricks for navigating uncertain times. That's what you'll find here in this daily reader: meditations, affirmations, questions for reflection, stories, and gentle nudges back to the Truth of who you are.

Every day you will receive a specific suggestion for what you can affirm, what you can ask yourself, how you can act, or how you can pray. You can, of course, just read the calendar day's entry, but you can also use the book as a divination tool, opening to a random page for an inspirational message. You can also make use of the index, browsing topics or searching for entries about a particular subject.

When we are overwhelmed by outer circumstances, the most powerful thing we can do is go within, do our own inner work, and tend to our own consciousness. This inner work influences the collective consciousness of the planet. Ultimately, there is only One Consciousness. It is God's Consciousness, and as expressions of the Divine—it is our consciousness, too.

So here is my deepest purpose: I want to see spiritual awareness on this planet rise dramatically—for you, for me, and for every single soul on earth. When this happens, I believe we will experience more peace, joy, love, and harmony than we have ever known. I think about this possibility every day, and I hope you will, too, as you read these pages.

No prior spiritual knowledge is required to enjoy this book. You'll find it speaks of an Infinite, Universal God, drawing from several faith traditions, with a strong foundation in New Thought spiritual principles, including ideas like the divine nature of humanity; the creative power of our thoughts; the interconnectedness of all life; the Law of Attraction; and the Truth of God's loving presence that permeates everything. If you are familiar with these concepts, may they uplift and inspire you anew. If these ideas are new to you, welcome! May they open your heart and awaken your spirit!

Here's to a year of good thoughts and spiritual growth!

Let's take this journey together—one day at a time.
Rev. Dr. Cynthia Paulsen

JANUARY

POSSIBILITY
JANUARY 1

Do you believe all things are possible? There is a power available to you that can change any negative, unwanted condition in your life, revealing peace, contentment, and purpose. Discovering this power for yourself may be your only job as a human being. You are an expression of this power. It goes by many names. Some call it God, Source, Allah, Brahman, Infinite Intelligence, the One Mind, or the One Life, but it doesn't matter what you call It. It just *is*, and because of It, all things are possible.

Begin this year, this day, this minute, by opening your mind to this idea. In this moment, open your life to the best possible experience you can imagine. This is a day of possibility!

Affirm

There is a power available to me that makes all things possible.

IMAGINE SOMETHING GOOD
JANUARY 2

Do you use your imagination for good, and not "evil"? When we visualize negative experiences and outcomes we don't want, we get negative experiences and outcomes that we don't want! We do this all the time, like planning arguments with someone in our head, fearing a bad experience at the doctor's office, or expecting bad news when the phone rings. We have to be aware of what we're imagining and do it consciously, in order to create our good.

Humanity in general tends to visualize conflict in the world. Imagine if we all actively spent time imagining and visualizing people living in harmony and peace. From the human perspective (as opposed to the spiritual perspective), we might think that's boring, but it's not. It's wonderful! Imagine the life you want. Visualize the world you want to live in—the harmony, the peace, the love. If we don't visualize what it can look like and be like, how can we expect it to happen? If we can experience it in our minds, we can experience it in our real-life conditions. Spiritual Law tells us that manifest form follows our invisible thought.

Ask

What good things can I imagine today?

IT IS YOU, TOO
JANUARY 3

How do you describe God (or whatever you like to call the One Power and Presence of the Infinite)? Maybe you would say things like:

> God is Unconditional Love.
> God is Peace.
> God is Harmony
> God is Wisdom.
> God is Joy.
> God is Wholeness.

These are all wonderful traits and qualities of God. Did you know that all these words that you would use to describe God can also be used to describe yourself? What is true of God is also true of you. Like produces like, or as the Bible says, "that which is born of Spirit is Spirit," (John 3:6). God, which is perfect, creates all life, which is also perfect. This is you, manifested perfection. All the potential of the God-Source is implanted within you.

Affirm

What is true of God is also true of me. God's nature is my nature.

SOMEWHERE IN THE CIRCLE
JANUARY 4

There is an iPhone utilities app called Find Me that allows people to share their GPS location. My husband and I use it, especially when one of us is traveling on a road trip alone. Sometimes, the app doesn't work right. Whether it is due to poor cell phone service or the app simply doesn't refresh properly, an exact location cannot be given. Instead, the phone is only able to give an approximate location. It shows you a circle on a map that encompasses several miles, and it says the person you are looking for is "somewhere in the circle." The vagueness of it always makes me chuckle. It isn't very helpful, but I suppose it is good to know a general location, if nothing else.

Perhaps this is where we can start with our understanding of God. Imagine that everywhere you go, always, there is a giant circle around you, extending out for miles. This circle follows you everywhere you go. The truth is, God is somewhere in the circle. Always. Stop searching. Stop trying to refresh. Stop spinning your wheels trying to pinpoint. Just know and trust that the presence of the Divine is there—always close by, always near, always within you.

Affirm

*The One Power, One Life, One Infinite Intelligence of God
is forever within my circle.*

ONE
JANUARY 5

Consider the concept of opposites: Light and darkness. Hot and cold. Big and little. There is actually no such thing as opposites. There is only one of everything. Hot and cold are just variations of one thing: temperature. Big and little are variations of size. Light and darkness are just various aspects of One Life. Darkness is simply the absence of light.

Imagine you have a completely dark, sealed off room with no windows and no light. You can't see anything. But, if you bring in just a little flickering candle, eventually, your eyes will adjust to the light of its flame, and you will begin to see what is in the room. The darkness is completely overpowered and eliminated by the light. The light is all that is real.

Affirm

There is only One Power, One Life, One Light.
It doesn't matter what I call It. This One Life just is.

FACTS VS. TRUTH
JANUARY 6

Spiritually, there is a difference between facts and truth. Facts are the conditions of our life, and they are the manifested effects of our thought. Truth (capital-T-Truth) is a divine reality. It's what Source intends for and expresses as in your life.

Truth is unchangeable. Truth is our divine nature, whether we are experiencing it in our current life conditions or not. A fact might be a doctor telling you that you have high blood pressure, but the Truth is the perfect health and wholeness that has the potential to express in your physical body. A fact might be that two countries are at war, but the Truth is the perfect love, peace, and harmony that exists within all people in both countries, wanting and willing to express. The Divine Truth is what we know deep down to be real, even when we can't see it. It is always possible, in any given moment, to realize the Truth.

Affirm

Today, I choose to keep my awareness on the Divine Truth.

A GOOD RECEIVER
JANUARY 7

Scripture tells us that we reap what we sow; the amount we give determines the amount we get back. This Law of Circulation is a spiritual principle based on giving and receiving. Receiving is just as much a part of the process as giving. It's not gluttonous, selfish, or greedy to receive your good. Are you a good receiver?

Open hands help facilitate the Law of Circulation in both directions. We can have hands that are open and ready to give, and hands that are open and ready to receive. If we are clutching at things, holding on too tightly to what we have while we're trying to receive our good, it doesn't work. Closed fists are not in a state of open flow.

Sometimes, this means we have to make room for our good, both mentally and physically. When we create a state of emptiness or lack, nature (Spiritual Law) will immediately move to fill it. Getting ready to receive means creating space mentally, by being still, quieting our thoughts, meditating, praying, etc. We create space physically by making room for our good that is coming our way. That means looking around our lives to see where we need to make some room. That can look like cleaning out a closet, moving a piece of furniture out of your house, spending some of the money in your wallet, or donating items to charity. The Law of Circulation does not expect you to give without receiving somewhere, somehow!

Ask

What can I let go of and release in order to receive my good?

GREAT EXPECTATIONS
JANUARY 8

Many people think of faith as "faith in God," or "faith in Jesus," or faith in some kind of religion, and there is nothing wrong with that! Faith can also be our belief about anything—our belief about ourselves, our belief about other people, or our belief about the world in which we live. Faith is what we regularly think and expect will happen. Do you have a confident expectancy of good in your life?

When you go to the Department of Motor Vehicles, do you expect long lines, angry people, and rude employees? That's what you are putting your faith in. Maybe you expect a pleasant experience and a good outcome? That is what you put your faith in. Putting your faith in good expectations is how you create good experiences.

Ask

What do I expect will happen in my daily experiences?

ABUNDANCE IN NATURE
JANUARY 9

Divine abundance is limitless and available to all. It is only our ability to receive that influences our lack or surplus. We, through our thoughts and beliefs, are the only ones who can limit our abundance and prosperity. God, the source of all resources, does not withhold anything. Is the ocean concerned about running out of water? Do plants worry about a lack of sunshine? We need only look to nature to see an abundance of giving, receiving, flowing, and growing. Even in times of extremes—flooding, drought, fire, storms—we see the eventual return to balance and restoration. This is what nature does. This is what the abundance of *Life* does.

There is enough for all, including you. Can you let go of your limiting thoughts? They do not serve you. Better still, can you replace them with abundant thoughts of expansion, plenty, and unexpected good?

Affirm

I am part of the abundant nature of Life. There is always enough.

AFFIRM GOOD HEALTH
JANUARY 10

Affirmations are short statements that remind us of our Divine Truth, and they are repeated or written down daily as a way to bring about positive transformation. They might be about something we want to change, or something we wish to have, do, or be.

Everyone wants and deserves to live a vibrant, healthy life free from disease and illness. If your health could use some improvement, write an affirmation about your health, or focus on one of these today.

Affirm

- *I make healthy choices every day.*
- *My body knows exactly what it needs to be healthy.*
- *Because I exist in perfect balance, I live harmoniously.*
- *I am worthy of a mentally stable, emotionally healthy life.*
- *Divine energy flows through me.*
- *Every cell in my body thrives with positive energy.*
- *Health is the natural state of my being.*
- *I choose to be healthy and free.*
- *I am perfect, whole, and complete.*

THANK YOU FOR THE GOOD
JANUARY 11

Did you know you can use the spiritual practice of gratitude when you aren't feeling well? The next time you feel sick and are experiencing physical symptoms in your body, shift your attention to what is working well in your body and give thanks for it. For instance, if you had a head cold and you were experiencing sinus congestion, you could stop and ask yourself: What is working well in my body? Can you still see? Are your eyes working? Do your legs work? Can you walk? Is your heart beating?

What this practice does is shift your attention away from negative things you don't want to be feeling to having appreciation and gratitude for what is working well in your body instead. It is shifting your attention to the good.

Affirm

The more I see the good and appreciate it, the more good I experience.

AS WE BELIEVE
JANUARY 12

Scripture tells us it is done unto us *as we believe* (Matt. 8:13). Our thoughts and beliefs create our experience, but it can be challenging to be aware of our thoughts all the time. When you notice a thought, stop and ask yourself: "Would God think this thought? Would God feel this way? Is this really true?" Asking yourself these questions helps you see when your thoughts might be out of alignment with your divine spiritual Truth.

Remember that when a thought is causing you pain, you can choose to stop thinking it! Instead of thinking something negative about your health, work, relationships, or finances, what spiritually inspiring, positive thoughts can you think instead? Can you affirm the Truth of your good health, your abundant life, and your loving encounters with family, friends, and strangers?

Affirm

*It is done unto me as I think and believe, not anyone else.
I get to choose, and I choose good thoughts.*

ALL PATHS/NO PATH
JANUARY 13

God is more infinite than any human mind can conceive. Who are we to limit the Divine to one religion, one faith tradition, or one spiritual experience? Perhaps God is the truth that transcends all versions of itself, all manner of tradition. God is ultra-personal to humanity in the most universal sense.

Human beings need the freedom to seek the Divine in whatever path resonates with them. That includes no path! Atheism, for instance, could be considered the spiritual path of no path, the right to seek the Divine in secular ways. That may sound strange, but when we expand our perception of God as broadly as possible, we help demonstrate the unity and oneness of all life.

Affirm

It's all God, and it's all good.

POWERFUL WORDS
JANUARY 14

Many spiritual traditions teach that creation was spoken into existence by the word. Indeed, we know the power of not only our thoughts and beliefs, but of our written and spoken word. A key point to remember is:

The more you believe your words are powerful,
The more powerful your words become.

If every word you spoke, wrote, and thought created your next experience, you would certainly make sure to speak, write, and think positive, abundant, life-affirming words. You would be mindful to never speak harshly or negatively of yourself or others. Take this concept to a diary or journal.

Ask

What can I write about my life? My desires? My dreams?

ABOUT SIN
JANUARY 15

Many people believe that *sin* is about our behavior—bad choices that supposedly go against God. "To sin" just means to miss the mark, like an archer who misses the target of a bullseye. It means to miss the point of human existence. When we sin, we are really just off track with our thinking and believing. We are likely lost in our human fears, thinking negatively about our life, holding on to false beliefs, and forgetting the Truth of our divinity.

Let's relax on judging our behavior (not to mention the behavior of others) and remember to stay aligned with the Divine. That means knowing our wholeness, our harmony, our love, our peace, our abundance, etc. You are only "sinning" when you forget that God is expressing in you, through you, and as you.

Affirm

A sin is simply a mistake in thought. I am allowed to make mistakes. The truth is, I am divine.

WHERE ARE YOU?
JANUARY 16

If asked, "Where are you right now?" everyone reading this would have a different answer. But every person can answer truthfully and accurately: "I am here." Each one of us is *here*, wherever that may be.

What does it mean to be *here* from a New Thought perspective? To be *here* means to be present. Alive. Awake. Aware. Conscious. Mindful. Receptive to the Divine. Tuned in to our inherent connection with Source. Wherever we are, that's where *here* is. *Here* is where life is, and *Life* is just another word for God, Spirit, Universe, or Source.

Life is showing up right here as *you*. Let this be an exercise in mindfulness. Be here now.

Ask

Where am I? Am I lost somewhere in an ego-based human experience, or am I alive in my awareness of God?

YOU ARE DIVINE
JANUARY 17

What does it mean to be "divine"? Before there were humans and animals, before there were plants and trees and oceans and land, before the earth was formed, and before the sun began to shine, when there were only floating bits of stars around, there was energy in motion. There was movement. There was Intelligence. There was God (or whatever you call the One Power, One Presence, One Life). Within this One Power was the idea of you. YOU! Your soul was there with God way back then, just like God is here now with you.

You can't be separated from this One Divine Power. That pulsing spark of energy that created the universe, the galaxies, the sun, the moon, the stars, and the earth, is within you now. It is beating your heart. It is firing the synapses in your brain. It is filling your lungs with air. The life force energy of God is expressing in you, through you, and as you. You matter. You are loved. You are divine.

Affirm

In this moment, I am aware that I am divine.

ON FAITH
JANUARY 18

Faith is a thing of thought. It takes place in our mind. It is a way of thinking and expecting, whether we are thinking good thoughts and expecting good things, or we're thinking negative thoughts based on false beliefs and expecting bad things. It is two sides to the same coin, but it's all faith. We have the opportunity every day to use our faith in a positive way that reveals our good. Consider what you are putting your faith in.

Affirm

I use my faith to create the life I want to experience.

THE WORK OF PEACE
JANUARY 19

Everyone wants world peace, but how many are willing to work for it? The work of peace begins with each one of us individually. A famous prayer by Chinese philosopher Lao Tzu reminds us:

> *If there is to be peace in the world,*
> *There must be peace in the nations.*
> *If there is to be peace in the nations,*
> *There must be peace in the cities.*
> *If there is to be peace in the cities,*
> *There must be peace between neighbors.*
> *If there is to be peace between neighbors,*
> *There must be peace in the home.*
> *If there is to be peace in the home,*
> *There must be peace in the heart.*

It isn't about marching in the streets, taking up arms, or gathering in protest. Doing the work of peace means cultivating the peace within you. Live, move, and have your being in the Peace of God. It is who and what you are in your heart, at the center of your being.

Act

Sit in the stillness. Be quiet. Show up as peace.
Let the Spirit of God lead you to express as the peace that you are.

MY DIVINE NATURE
JANUARY 20

God's Divine Nature is my nature.
God's Love is my love.
God's Peace is my peace.
God's Joy is my joy.
God's Wholeness is my wholeness.
God's Abundance is my abundance.
God's Creativity is my creativity.
God's Balance is my balance.
God's Freedom is my freedom.
God's Consciousness is my consciousness.

You get the idea. When we deny our divine nature, we live in limitation until we change our thinking. You have the opportunity, every day, every moment, to express as the limitless nature of God.

Where in your life can you open your mind to these Truths? What other Divine Truths are you longing to claim for yourself? You are not trapped. You are not restricted. You are not limited.

Affirm

It is only my thinking and my beliefs that limit me.
God's Nature is my nature.

SPEAK THE NEW THOUGHT
JANUARY 21

Once we recognize that a thought is false and no longer serving us, what do we do next? We release it! More importantly, we use our free will to think a new thought.

Sometimes this literally looks like thinking and affirming the opposite of what we had been thinking before. It may feel clunky, unnatural, and strange at first. Affirm the new thought anyway! Choose to speak in a new way about your life. Claim your highest good, even before you see it. Let the truth of a divinely guided, spiritually aligned thought take over your consciousness. Everything you could possibly want is within you.

Affirm

*I release false thoughts that do not serve me.
I am ready to speak the Truth of my life!*

LIFT YOUR CONSCIOUSNESS
JANUARY 22

Even a brief look at world events reported in the news makes us realize how challenging it is to remain spiritually positive and uplifted, focused on the good. How can we do this when such awful things are happening in the world? Scary news days are a great reminder that each one of us has the opportunity to show up in the world as peace, radiating peace in all our daily interactions.

We always have the free will to consciously refuse to engage and participate in days filled with difficult news, accounts of violence, or generally heartbreaking information. If you see hatred in the world, you can concentrate on the truth that God is Love, and therefore, you are love. If there is sadness in the world, you can know that God is Joy, and therefore, you are an expression of that joy. If there is violence in the world, you can remember that God is Peace, and you are an expression of peace.

Choose to lift your consciousness in these moments. Choose to remember the Truth of who and what you are. You are divine.

Affirm

*No matter what happens in the news,
I am the opportunity to show up as the Divine.*

PLAY TIME
JANUARY 23

Parents of young children know all too well the importance of play. Children learn by playing with others and by themselves. It helps them learn social skills and grow mentally and physically. Recess is an important part of the school day. Play is also FUN! Is there a more beautiful sound than children laughing and playing outside on a warm sunny day?

As adults, play is rarely prioritized. When was the last time you played make-believe, a sport, or even a board game? When was the last time you laughed until you cried? Joy is a very high vibrational frequency that improves our health and lifts our spirit. Consciously choosing to seek joy through joyful activities like play helps us live more in alignment with Source.

Ask

Where can I play and choose joy today?

MIRACLE TALK
JANUARY 24

Are you entitled to miracles?
As a child of the Divine, the answer is yes.

Will you receive miracles?
As a child of the Divine, the answer is yes.

Do you offer miracles?
As a child of the Divine, the answer is yes.

If your answer is no to any of these questions, remember that you are one with God. You operate in the same creative way as the Divine.

Affirm

I am a child of God, and I am entitled to miracles.
I deserve miracles, and I expect to receive miracles.
I am God's opportunity to show up every day as a miracle.

A PRAYER FOR THE WORLD
JANUARY 25

Prayer is energy and frequency, and it makes a difference in this chaotic world. Join me in knowing the Truth.

Pray

There is only One Power, One Presence, One Life. Some people call it Spirit, Source, or the Universe. It doesn't matter what we call It because this One Life just <u>is</u>. I call It God, and I know It to be good and only good. I know God's nature is Peace, Harmony, and Love. I know I am one with these qualities and these traits, that God's nature is my nature. It is your nature as well. It is the nature of all life. Nothing can separate us from this Truth. There is no war in God. There is no chaos. There is only Oneness, Unity, Harmony, Peace, and Love.

I know with certainty that deep down in the heart of all those involved in any human conflict lies God's Truth. At the center of it all is love. I know love overcomes all fear, violence, and pain. This is possible because all things are possible. I am focused on love, peace, and the possibility of miracles. I am seeking and trusting in the goodness of life. This is mine to do in this moment. This is the Truth that is mine to know. I give great thanks for life and for all the unique ways that Spirit shows up in this world. I am thankful for the spiritually aware, the peacemakers, and the power of prayer. I allow this shift in my consciousness, fully expecting and anticipating expressions of peace and harmony and love in the world. I let this go with great reverence and gratitude.

And So It Is. Amen.

USE YOUR PATH
JANUARY 26

There are countless deeply personal ways to connect with the Divine, such as prayer, meditation, chanting, journaling, daily rituals, walking in nature, reading sacred texts, breathwork, religious worship, and more. We can practice any method we want to connect with and feel close to God. We do what makes sense and works for us individually. What *doesn't* make sense is to judge another person's spiritual path. A famous Hindu proverb says:

> "There are hundreds of paths up the mountain, all leading to the same place. It doesn't matter which path you take. The only person wasting time is the one who runs around the mountain, telling everyone that his or her path is wrong."

Rather than spending energy deciding whether someone else's path is right or wrong, we can focus on our own. How is your spiritual path looking these days? Sometimes we outgrow a spiritual practice the way we outgrow a pair of shoes. What once fit and worked perfectly might one day feel tight or uncomfortable. It doesn't mean anything is wrong; it might just mean it is time to try something new. Again, we do what works for us, and there are so many choices. Find your path and enjoy it!

Ask

What spiritual practice currently nourishes me?
Is there another one I am curious to explore?

POPCORN TIMING
JANUARY 27

Have you ever made old-fashioned popcorn in a pot on the stove? You heat oil, pour in the kernels, put on the lid, and wait. The kernels burst open at different times, unpredictably. Sometimes, they never pop at all. Why is that? Popcorn kernels pop when the moisture inside them turns to steam. Steam creates pressure against the hard outer shell until it bursts open, causing the starch to expand, turn inside out, and solidify into the snack we call popcorn. The process fluctuates because of variations in moisture content, hull strength, and how evenly each kernel absorbs the heat. There are so many variables! There is no single cause that initiates a pop for each kernel.

Popcorn is a metaphor for our journey toward spiritual awareness. Each of us is on a spiritual path, gradually "heating up" through life experiences. Filled with enthusiasm for spiritual growth, some seem to burst open quickly. Others appear uninterested or resistant. We all carry our past experiences with us —good or bad—and we respond to life differently.

Spiritual awakening does not follow a universal timeline. We each gain understanding in our own time, in our own unique way. Some may never consciously arrive at an awakened sense of completion. That, too, is part of the mystery of life! The deeper lesson is: don't compare your journey to anyone else's. Trust the process. Everything happens in divine timing.

Affirm

There is no reason to judge anyone's level of spiritual understanding, including my own. I learn, grow, and expand in God's perfect timeline.

POSSIBILITY OF PEACE
JANUARY 28

In Mark 9:23, Jesus said, "Everything is possible for one who believes." It doesn't say *some* things are possible. It says everything. It doesn't say everything is possible *for one who believes in a certain spiritual path or a certain religious denomination.* It's not about that. It's about our belief. It is always about our belief in the possibility we wish to experience. Do we believe it is possible?

This spiritual Truth can be used for and by the collective, especially regarding war and world conflicts. Do you believe peace is possible? Go there, in your heart, in your mind, in your meditation, and in your prayer. Think about it, imagine it, and believe it. This is how we bring about peace, by believing strongly in the possibility that it can happen.

Affirm

I believe in the possibility of peace, and I expect to see peace in my world.

LET IT BE
JANUARY 29

There is a beautiful song by the Beatles called "Let It Be," and the lyrics convey a wonderful metaphysical message. It is beneficial for us to let our human problems be, and to hear the words of wisdom deep within our soul—to know the Truth of who we are. No matter what the conditions of your life might look like, you can let them be because the truth is your soul is the perfect wisdom of the great, Infinite Intelligence of God. That is our Truth.

What human problems, concerns, and worries can you "let be" for a while? How can you practice this?

Act

Stop talking about your problems.
Stop worrying.
Sit in the stillness and know the Truth.
Let it be.

HOW ARE YOU VIBRATING?
JANUARY 30

Both physics and philosophy teach that everything is energy. This includes human thoughts and emotions. High-vibration energy frequencies are associated with happiness, positivity, and joy. Low-vibration frequencies are associated with negative emotions, like shame, sadness, guilt, and fear. Humans have free will to decide what state of mind we wish to be in and how we want to feel. We can control this, and we are responsible for our state of mind. Our thoughts, beliefs, and attitudes constantly influence our vibrational frequency. The more we are aware of this, the easier it is to enjoy life from a high-frequency, high consciousness level.

Affirm

*My mind, body, and spirit are vibrating in the
highest, healthiest, happiest, and most harmonious frequency.*

EVERYWHERE AT ALL TIMES
JANUARY 31

Divine Science teaches the Omnipresence of God. The foundation of the teaching is that whatever you call it—the One Power, One Presence, One Life of God is equally present everywhere at all times. That means in this moment, right now, God is here. Source is present. Life is here, flowing, existing, expressing as your individual personality. You have the free will to be aware of this, and to consciously choose to live in alignment with any and all Source qualities.

Act

Slow down, and consider this:
because you are here, God is here.

FEBRUARY

WE ARE THE ESSENCE
FEBRUARY 1

A famous quote by the poet Rumi says: "You are not a drop in the ocean; you are the entire ocean in a drop." It helps us understand the magnitude of our unity with Source. We are each, individually, the drop. God is the ocean. We are not a tiny part of God; we are all of God's essence in our own tiny drop of existence.

Another metaphor for this concept is the vine and the branches scripture that Jesus taught. "I am the vine, you are the branches" (John 15:5). A branch isn't the entire tree, but it is made from everything the tree is. A branch has the same qualities and traits as the tree. The branch can't exist apart from the tree. They are one.

Yet another explanation of this is the chocolate cake metaphor. Picture a big, round chocolate cake as the God-Source. We are each a slice of chocolate cake. We are not God, but we are the essence of God. All the ingredients, flavors, and textures of the whole cake are in the slice—in us. The essence is there. We are not all that God is, but all that God is exists in us.

Affirm

The divine qualities of God are expressing in me.
I am expressing as the One Power, One Presence, and One Life of God.

LET IT SETTLE
FEBRUARY 2

If you have a cup of dirty water filled with rocks, mud, and grit, one way to clean it is to let it settle. You put the cup down and let it be still and calm. Eventually, the dirt falls to the bottom of the cup. The longer you let it sit, the more the dirt and tiny sediments fall to the bottom, and the clearer the water becomes.

This is a great metaphor for our spiritual life. It is always a good idea to be still, to be calm, to let your thoughts clear, to practice the pause, and to breathe. Consider it an opportunity to get clear and remember your Truth, the truth that God is all there is, good and only good. It is through that clarity that we realize we are one with this goodness and cannot be separated from God, no matter what we are experiencing.

We are, each of us, an eternal soul, expressing in a human body for a time. When we are still, we recognize the good unfolding in our lives, and we can move into a space of gratitude for it all.

Act

Take a moment today to be still and let it settle.

PERCEIVING A PROBLEM
FEBRUARY 3

There is a difference between seeing as God sees and seeing how we see as a human being. When we are experiencing something negative like lack, sickness, or loneliness, it is helpful to ask ourselves, "Is the difficulty in the condition, or is it in my seeing?" Could the problem be your perception or misconception of the situation?

If we understand that God can bring forth only perfection, then whatever we're experiencing is, by nature, perfect—if we choose to see it that way and believe it to be so. If we believe that God is present in all creation, then if we are having problems, it might be our wrong conception of the situation.

Two things to remember:

1. This is not about blame; it is an opportunity for understanding.
2. It is challenging to think in this way. Give yourself grace. In this moment, circle back to what you know to be true. God's intelligent, powerful, loving, harmonious, capital-L-Life is in action in all your experience at all times.

Affirm

*I choose to understand my life experiences
from a place of love and compassion.
God's perfection is at the center of my being.*

BEYOND FORGIVENESS
FEBRUARY 4

Forgiveness is for our own benefit, so that we are not carrying old hurts and suffering from the past. It helps us experience peace. Forgiveness does not mean we have to have a relationship with the person we are forgiving, though. This can be challenging for families, especially when we are related to the person whom we might need to forgive or who may need to forgive us. Even if we get to the point where past hurts are forgiven, that doesn't necessarily mean we can be comfortable around them or want to be close with them.

Consider taking forgiveness a step further with these ideas: Mentally wish the person well. Then make the decision to wish for them the same good that you wish for your own life. Want that for them just because they are another human being, a child of God. Try to imagine good things happening to them. Can you get yourself to a place where you can be happy about their happiness? This is a deep forgiveness practice.

Affirm

I am able to forgive.

WEB OF LIFE
FEBRUARY 5

You are a pulsing point of light in the giant network that is life. You are an expression of God's light in this infinite web of connections. We are all connected. We are all one; all loved by the same Source. As St. Augustine once said, "God loves each of us as if there were only one of us." For a split second after reading those words, it all makes sense. We are all just one, and THAT is what God loves.

Interacting with your fellow human beings is an opportunity for divine networking. Every person you meet is a chance to discover a unique aspect of God. When I go to the place in my mind where I recognize the love, peace, and wholeness that is within me, and you do the same within you, it is as if we meet there together. That is how we use the web of life to network and connect with one another.

Ask

Can I access the web of life in a loving, harmonious way, on a regular basis, even with people who look, act, and think differently than I do?

MAKE IT BIGGER
FEBRUARY 6

Think about God for a moment (whatever your understanding of God might be). Think about the best qualities and traits of the Divine: unconditional love, perfect harmony, absolute peace, limitless power, complete wholeness, infinite intelligence, unending creativity, deep wisdom, everlasting joy, etc. Hold these thoughts in your mind.

Now, imagine that the Divine is actually bigger and better than what you were just thinking. Imagine God to be more encompassing, more unifying, more universal, and more wonderful than we can grasp in our tiny little human brains. Think about this throughout your day:

Ask

How can I make my understanding of God bigger, wider, deeper, and more far-reaching?

DO SOMETHING NEW
FEBRUARY 7

One of the definitions of life is the capacity for growth, activity, and continual change. Life is movement, animation, and expansion. Our spiritual development is part of this. Our purpose here, as human beings, is to evolve. It does not serve us to be stagnant. Learn something new. Study something you have never heard of. Read something you are unfamiliar with. Experience something you have never experienced. We are here to grow spiritually. Life, on both the soul and human level, is an eternal progression. Expand your horizons.

Affirm

I am always ready to learn and grow spiritually.
I say yes to experiencing more life today!

ABOVE THE CLOUDS
FEBRUARY 8

Sometimes your flight takes off from the airport in gloomy, rainy weather. As the plane climbs in altitude, you suddenly see sunshine and clear blue skies outside the window above the clouds. The entire flight is smooth and enjoyable, and the plane approaches your destination. Upon the plane's descent through more clouds, you discover it is cloudy and gloomy in the city in which you are arriving.

This experience is a great metaphor for our spiritual life. Behind all our dark "human" moments, our gloomy days, our difficult, challenging life conditions, lies the Truth of our unity with Spirit, the Truth of God's goodness and light. It is always there behind the clouds. The reality of our eternal life and the spiritual perfection of our soul is our constant, unchangeable Truth.

Act

Stay focused on what exists above the clouds!

IT COULD GO RIGHT
FEBRUARY 9

Are you someone who spends your time worrying about things that could happen? Do you complain about things that haven't happened, but in your mind, they *might* happen? Are you always thinking about things that could go wrong? Here is a new thought to think. Ask yourself, "What if it all goes *right*?" What if you spent time thinking about and imagining *that* scenario instead?

Instead of wasting time worrying about what could go wrong, you can just as easily think and believe that everything could go right in your life. That outcome is just as possible; it can all work out. All could be well in your experience. It takes the same amount of time and the same amount of effort. The next time you find yourself worrying about something, stop and ask yourself, "What if nothing goes wrong? What if it all goes right? What if it is better than I expected?"

Affirm

Today, I choose to give my attention
to only the best possible outcomes I wish to see.

SPEAK GOD'S LANGUAGE
FEBRUARY 10

Praying from a place of want, a sense of need, or a feeling of lack often doesn't get good results. The reason it doesn't work is because God doesn't know what any of those things are. How could God understand want, need, or lack, when God is unlimited abundance and infinite good? How can we expect God to answer our prayers if we aren't even speaking the same language?

Affirmative Prayer, or Spiritual Mind Treatment, speaks the language of God. It speaks the language of our true divine nature. No matter what the world of appearances might look like, no matter what the condition is that we are experiencing that is motivating us to pray, we cannot be disturbed by it. We must be firmly rooted in our unity with Spirit and affirm our Divine Truth—our peace, love, joy, abundance, health, and well-being.

Affirm

I choose to speak the language of spiritual Truth.

STEPS OF AFFIRMATIVE PRAYER
FEBRUARY 11

Affirmative Prayer (Spiritual Mind Treatment) involves thinking and believing things already are as you would prefer them to be. There are five steps to this kind of prayer process:

Recognition - You recognize that God is all there is. One Power, One Presence, One Life, regardless of what someone calls it.

Unification - You unify yourself with this Power. It is understanding you are one with this Power and Presence. You live, move, and have your being in It.

Realization - This is the juicy part, the "why" you are praying at this moment. You realize and declare the Truth of what the experience is you desire, whether you see it happening yet or not. For instance, maybe you are praying because you are sick, feeling miserable, and want to be healed. This is where you deny that sickness has any power over you, and you realize and declare the Truth that you are healthy and whole in God. Spiritually, you are perfect; therefore, you expect to see an out picturing of your perfect health in physical form. You speak your Truth and talk about this good until you believe it fully. You want to shift your consciousness to a place of belief.

Thanksgiving - Self-explanatory, this is giving thanks for it all, that this is the way the Infinite Intelligence of God works. You can give thanks for answered prayer.

Release - You let it go, spiritually, trusting it is done. Be content that it is done. Proclaim, "And So It Is. Amen."

Act

Write your own Affirmative Prayer about your life following these steps.

GENERAL HEALTH TREATMENT
FEBRUARY 12

Affirmative Prayer/Spiritual Mind Treatment does not have to be flowery, overly complicated, or excessively long. For instance, a treatment for general health, well-being, and goodness in your life might look like this:

Pray

I recognize that God is all there is, and God is good and only good.
I understand that I am one with God. My ever-present good surrounds me.
Whatever the outcome and Truth I wish to experience, I claim it as my good, right here and now. I am healthy and happy. All is well in my life and in all my affairs.
I am grateful for all the ways God's Truth unfolds in my experience.
Releasing this prayer, I let this go, trusting and expecting its fulfillment.
And So It Is. Amen.

IT IS TESTABLE
FEBRUARY 13

The object of Affirmative Prayer is to be so focused on the Presence of God, so unified with Spirit, and therefore aligned with our Truth, that we cannot help but manifest our highest good and best life experience. It will naturally unfold and be revealed with no effort on our part because that's the way Spiritual Law works.

Remember, *we* are not doing the work when we pray affirmatively. We don't have to create or manifest anything. Spirit does the work, and It is simply revealing to us what is already there. We are using the power that is within us, as Jesus taught and modeled. Our experience is the outcome of our inner vision, what we believe and affirm. Affirmative Prayer treatments can be played with, tried, and tested. You can see for yourself what using this kind of language and following these steps does for your life.

Affirm

I choose today to have fun with Affirmative Prayer!

BE SWEET
FEBRUARY 14

Valentine's Day makes us think of love. Everywhere you go, in all the stores, you see the pink flowers, the red hearts, and the corny, mushy material displays of romance. When we resist the urge to be cynical, these displays are wholesome, charming, and sweet. Valentine's Day is a day to be consciously aware of our love. It is an opportunity to choose to be generous and sweet with it. But can't we choose to do this every day?

How can you be generous with your innate loving presence? Can you consciously use the love that is within you in sweet ways? Could you have a loving attitude as you walk down the grocery store aisle? Can you smile lovingly as you wave to a neighbor across the street? Can you call a friend, engage with an acquaintance, or compliment a stranger? We attract love when we allow ourselves to be love. It is the Truth of our being.

Affirm

Today and every day, I choose to show up as Divine Love.

FEEL THE JOY
FEBRUARY 15

We know that everything is energy. Have you ever walked in a room where people are arguing or laughing, and you could immediately sense the energy of the space? Different emotions have different vibrational energetic frequencies. There is truth to the idea that the better we feel, meaning the better emotions that we are feeling, the more aligned we are with the God-Source. Low-vibration emotions like fear, grief, and despair are the emotions we would feel when we are feeling separate from Source. High-vibration emotions like love, appreciation, and empowerment are the emotions we feel when we know the Truth of our wholeness in God. The highest vibrational emotion that most aligns us with the God-Source is joy.

Tragic world events often seem heavy, and it can feel challenging to be in a place of joy and feel good when devastating news gets us down. This is a reminder to consciously and actively seek joy in your life—something that makes you laugh and smile. Seek out something that makes you feel good to realign yourself with the Divine.

Affirm

Today, I remember to vibrate high and seek joy.

GOT A COLD?
FEBRUARY 16

A Spiritual Mind Treatment/Affirmative Prayer for healing from a cold and congestion:

Pray

Join with me in knowing the Truth that God is all there is. There is One Power, One Presence, One Life. I call it God, but it doesn't matter what we call it because this Power just is. It is good and only good. I know this Power and Presence and Life of God to express as Harmony, Wholeness, and Health, and I know that God's nature is my nature. I live, and move, and have my being in this power in this presence. My body expresses as Harmony, Wholeness, and Health. I know that this is within the realm of possibility. I know when I feel symptoms, when I feel feverish, when I have a cough, when there is congestion in my lungs, when I am not feeling well, I understand that this is not my Truth! These symptoms have no power over my life.

I turn within to the spiritual perfection and wholeness that I know is my Truth. I know that every cell within my body, every organ in my body, can operate as the spiritual perfection it is meant to be. Optimal wellness is being activated as these words are spoken. This is what I say YES to! This is what I give thanks for. I am so grateful that in my mind, body, spirit, and soul, I am open and ready to express as wholeness. There is nothing to heal, only a revelation to unfold, and I am ready. I give great thanks for the Creative Process and for Spiritual Law. I am so thankful that every time this prayer is read, the energy of it reaches out and healing spreads. I release these words into the action of the Law, knowing it is so, fully expecting and anticipating its fulfillment.

And So It Is. Amen

YOUR SNOWFLAKE EXPERIENCE
FEBRUARY 17

We have all heard the saying, "No two snowflakes are alike," but do you know the science behind it? Snowflakes are very sensitive to temperature, and because of this, they often change shape as they fall to the ground. Scientists believe that the likelihood of two snow crystals being identical is zero because it would be impossible for two snowflakes to have the exact same experience on their way to the ground.

One might carry this idea further and say that each snowflake is an individual, having its own experiences, living its own life, expressing in its own way. This is exactly what human beings do. We are unique in our individual choices, our experiences, our expression, yet we are all alike in and one with God. Think of yourself as an individualized center of God-consciousness, born to fulfill your divine purpose and express your Divine Truth in your own individual way. You are here to create something with your life that only *you* can do.

Affirm

I am an individualized expression of God,
here to create my best life and experience my highest good.

BREATHING
FEBRUARY 18

Do you have trouble practicing the pause, going within, or sitting in the silence? Sometimes it seems humans just aren't wired for contemplative stillness. They call it "spiritual practice" for a reason; it takes effort and practice. One tip is to focus on your breathing, something we normally give no thought to. When we suddenly pay attention to our breathing and let that task consume us, it naturally quiets our mind.

Once your mind is quiet, use your inhale as a time to affirm something good about yourself, like, "I am peace," or "I am healthy," or "I breathe in love." On your exhale, you can do this as well, perhaps declaring, "All is well," or "Love is all there is," or "I release the past." How often can you do this practice? Do it as often as you need to experience peace.

Affirm

Today, I let breathing be my path to peace.

IT'S NOT ABOUT WORDS
FEBRUARY 19

Does the word *God* work for you? I often say, "God, Spirit, Universe, Source, or whatever word works for you." Some people don't like the word God because they associate it with negative church experiences or past religious trauma. The truth is, no one owns the word God. One particular religious group does not get to define God for all humanity. Far beyond the words, theologies, creeds, dogmas, and rituals of all religion lies the unlimited power, frequency, and energy of God. There are many other words that one could use in place of God. What do you call the One Power behind all that is? What if you had to call it something else? Would that bother you?

Remember, words (language in general) are a human construct. Spirit has no use for words. From a soul perspective, communication takes place through non-physical means, using symbols, emotions, signs, intuitions, visions, feelings, and natural phenomena. We are better off thinking of the Divine in these kinds of terms, instead of labeling It with words.

Affirm

*Today, I remember that my words don't actually matter;
my awareness of the Divine is all that matters.*

IT'S YOUR LIFE
FEBRUARY 20

You are free from limitation when you understand the Truth of your divine nature. Spirit can only create out of itself; therefore, you must be made of the same qualities of Spirit. In Divine Science* theology, this is called the Law of Expression, referencing the fact that like produces like, that which is born of Spirit is Spirit.

Your physical body and all your affairs are reflecting whatever level of consciousness you are feeling. The higher your consciousness (the alignment of your thoughts and beliefs with the Truth of God's perfect nature), the more you will see perfection, wholeness, and prosperity demonstrate in your life experience. This version of life is available to you simply because you exist. This life is the only life.

Affirm

God's Life is perfect, and it is my life now.

---

* James, F. B., & Cramer, M. E. (1957). *Divine Science; Its Principles and Practice. compiled from Truth and Health, by Fannie B. James and Divine Science and Healing, by Malinda E. Cramer*. Textbook of Divine Science.

ALWAYS LISTENING
FEBRUARY 21

Once, while spending the night at my daughter's apartment, I struggled to turn on the lights when it started to get dark. She had gone to work, and none of the light switches would work. I tried turning the switches on the lamps, and nothing happened. I was so frustrated sitting there in the dark! I texted her, and finally she called me on her break and told me, "I'm so sorry, I forgot to tell you! I have an Alexa. You just have to say, 'Alexa, turn on the lights!'" I felt so silly. It worked, of course, right away.

This is a beautiful illustration of how Spirit works. Just like how an Alexa™ is always listening, waiting for you to give the command and say the right words, Spirit is always listening, too. It is God's great pleasure to give us the kingdom—all of our desires, if we will only affirm and know the Divine Truth for ourselves and speak our word. Remember, Spirit is always listening.

Ask

Where in my life am I sitting in the dark,
forgetting that I can speak my word and turn on the light?

NEED A HUG?
FEBRUARY 22

When we repeatedly see news regarding global catastrophes, it activates our fight-or-flight state, triggering stress, fatigue, and emotional numbness. Our overwhelmed nervous systems need relief. It seems like humanity is in desperate need of a giant hug. What can we do to soothe ourselves? There is a simple practice you can do using your heart and your brain.

When we receive a long hug from someone we love, it triggers the release of oxytocin, dopamine, and serotonin, hormones that reduce stress, induce calmness, decrease anxiety, and increase feelings of happiness. But what if there isn't a person nearby to hug us? It turns out, we don't need another person to accomplish this. Place your hand on your chest over your heart and hold it there with gentle pressure for at least six seconds (or longer). Your brain cannot distinguish between an actual hug with another person and this act of self-soothing. It responds the same way, releasing the hormones, calming your nervous system.

Your body is divinely, intelligently designed, full of innate wisdom that constantly works to support you. You deserve comfort. You deserve to feel safe. You deserve a hug. Give yourself one.

Affirm

I am embraced by the Universe.
I am safe, supported, and deeply loved.

PEACEFUL ORDER
FEBRUARY 23

Life is orderly; just look at the way the planets orbit the sun in perfect order. Think about the exact science that can predict moon cycles and ocean tides. So often, our human lives feel chaotic, and world events seem out of our control. But chaos is not the Truth of how life works. Intelligent order is actually the law of life. This can be a very peaceful realization.

Peaceful order is our natural state of existence. Peace is who and what we are at our core, at the center of our being. No matter what is going on, no matter what conditions we are experiencing, no matter how chaotic the world looks, the reality is: there is peace.

Affirm

*No matter what I see, I know peaceful order is all around me,
moving through me, and existing in me.
I am the Peace of God in expression.*

SUPPORT IS THERE
FEBRUARY 24

God is the invisible partner in our lives, always. When we invite and allow it, we can recognize that we are loved, supported, and guided. There is always something deep in our soul—that which knows what decisions we ought to make—and how we should move forward in life. This is our awareness of our unity with the Divine. <u>We</u> might not know what to do next, but something (God within us) does know.

The truth is, we never need to feel confused, scared, worried, or unsure. We can decide, at any moment, to invite Source to direct our path and then listen to the guidance. With this assurance, we can know with certainty how to live our best life.

Affirm

*I am never alone. As long as I choose to believe it,
I am loved, supported, and guided.*

EXPECT DIVINE GUIDANCE
FEBRUARY 25

Have you ever had to come up with a creative idea or solve a problem, whether it be for work or in your personal life? Human beings have an incredible ability to be creative. How amazing it is to realize that the creative answers to any human problem already exist in Divine Mind. They are already there. It is our choice—our opportunity—to be in alignment with Source, to know our divine nature, to recognize the Omnipresence of God. This is when our creative thinking flows, and answers are revealed. Think of some problem or situation that you are dealing with in your life for which you would like guidance or a creative solution.

Affirm

I expect guidance in this endeavor.
I may not know how to solve this, but I know Spirit does.
I am open, willing, and ready to receive my divine answer!

WHAT IS CONSTANT?
FEBRUARY 26

Perhaps you have heard the saying, "The only thing that is constant is change." From a human perspective, this feels true. Life unfolds through growth, movement, expansion, and transition. We begin new chapters, leave others behind, and adapt again and again to changing circumstances.

There is something deeper and more reliable than change itself. God does not change. God is constant, stable, and trustworthy. While human conditions shift, God remains the same.

This is important to remember in times of transition like when we start a new job, move to a new home, enter or leave a relationship, welcome new life, grieve a loss, or step into an unknown season. Our life experience may feel uncertain, but the Presence of God is steady and sure. The One Power is operating in us, through us, and as us.

Our emotions may vary, and our circumstances may look different from one moment to the next, but the Mind of God within us never changes. When we remember our unity with God, we discover an inner stability that is not dependent on conditions. We are supported and guided, no matter where life takes us.

Affirm

*No matter what I experience,
I remain faithful, unmoved,
and unchanged because I am one with God.*

WHAT DOES YOUR BODY WANT?
FEBRUARY 27

Once, when a friend came to visit, I offered to make her some fresh juice. She asked what kind. I replied, "I can make beet juice, or I can make green juice. Which one would you like?" She proceeded to put her hand on her heart, close her eyes, and whisper softly to herself, "Do I want beet juice or green juice? Beet juice or green juice?" It was a spiritual practice ritual for her. She was pausing to connect with her physical expression—her divine body—to see what it wanted in that moment.

How often do you eat or drink whatever is in front of you without stopping to consider what your body actually wants? Another trick that same friend taught me is when out in a restaurant, browsing a menu, consciously pay attention to whether your mouth waters as you read a certain item. That might mean your body really wants that choice. These are great tips to stay in alignment with the physical expression of your body and know what it truly wants.

Ask

What does my body want right now?

A HUMAN BEING
FEBRUARY 28

When we are introduced to someone for the first time, after learning their name, we often ask, "What do you do?" (Everybody does something.) Humans are quite attached to our *doing*—our work, our productivity, and our busy-ness. Our jobs, hobbies, and activities are a big part of who we are and how we describe ourselves. Yet, an inspirational quote attributed to the Dalai Lama tells us, "You are a human being, not a human doing."

We have a choice, at any given moment, where we feel attachment and where we wish to put our attention. In this moment, shift your attention away from your *doing*. Ask yourself: *How am I being? If I am a human being, how then shall I be?*

Go within. *Be* still. *Be* peace. This is a conscious decision to make at this moment, to align with the Truth of your peaceful, divine nature. At the center of your being, you are peace.

Affirm

*Today, I choose to recognize I am a human being,
existing and expressing as Divine Peace.*

SOMETHING UNEXPECTED
FEBRUARY 29*

February 29th is a leap day added to calendars every four years. Most people don't keep track of which years are leap years, so when it happens, the day feels like an unexpected surprise. According to an old Irish legend, women are allowed to propose to men on leap day, supposedly to balance out the traditional roles of men and women (the same way leap day balances out the calendar). It is a different way of proposing marriage—a change from the "typical" way that process unfolds.

Leap day is a great day to do something—*anything*—differently than you normally do. Use today as an opportunity to be consciously aware of your life habits, routines, and decisions. What can you do differently, just for fun? Take a different route to work. Order a new coffee drink instead of your usual. Try out a new restaurant you have never been to. Surprise a friend with a visit. Play hooky from work or school. Let today be full of unexpected, different choices. Actively embrace change, big or small. At the end of the day, check in with yourself to see if you feel more balanced.

Affirm

I open myself to new experiences. I am balanced.

---

*If you're reading this on February 28th, March 1st, or any day other than leap day, consider permission granted to balance yourself out and do something unexpected!

MARCH

NOTHING IS TRULY LOST
MARCH 1

Have you ever lost something valuable, and you really wanted it back? When I lose something important, I go within and pray to remind myself that there is only One Mind, One Power, One Life, and it's God's Life. That Life is my life. I am a part of the One Mind of Spirit. Therefore, I know nothing can be lost in Spirit. I do my best to lift my consciousness to a place of alignment with that Truth, and I ask for the location of the missing item to be revealed to me. I declare my full expectation that the item is already on its way back to me. It works! I have had several missing items, including a necklace and wallet, returned to me in miraculous ways.

Affirm

Nothing can be lost in Spirit.

A METAPHOR FOR ABUNDANCE
MARCH 2

Imagine that you are standing in front of an enormous, vast ocean, and you are holding a tiny teacup to get your share of the water. That is all you are going to get—just a teacup full because that is the vessel you have brought. You could be holding a five-gallon plastic bucket like they sell at hardware stores. You could come to the ocean with a big wooden wine barrel, or, if you could lift it, a giant bathtub. How about a huge water tank? (That might be hard to carry.)

The point of this metaphor is that *we* are the only ones who limit our ability to receive, not Source. So, a question for you to consider is: How much good can you receive? The answer is always: as much as you can believe and prepare for! Your belief and your mental expectation are your vessel. Prepare the largest container you can imagine and believe in your abundance.

Affirm

My abundance is unlimited, and I am ready to receive!

TIME TO WAKE UP
MARCH 3

Are you awake to your reality? Of course you are awake to your human reality. You participate in life, interact with friends and family, contribute to society, earn a living, and function quite well. But what about the capital-R-Reality? Are you awake to that one? So many of us are asleep to this reality. No one can awaken you to your spiritual Truth; no one can do it for you. No one can choose the method and path of your awakening. Only you can make the conscious choice to allow the Infinite, Universal God-Source into your awareness.

Affirm

Today, I awaken to the Reality that I am an eternal soul, one with the Divine.

TRUST YOUR PARTNER
MARCH 4

You can decide today to put all your affairs in the Infinite Intelligence of God. You can decide to let your relationship with the Divine be a true partnership, where God leads and directs your thoughts with deep wisdom. Why worry and struggle with watching your thoughts and trying to manage your beliefs? Hand it off to your partner! Choose today to trust that your way is made clear, and no obstacle can possibly block your good. Meditate on these words.

Affirm

I am led by Spirit and guided by wisdom.
Right thinking comes easily and effortlessly.
I am in partnership with God, fully loved and supported in every way.

UNDERNEATH IT ALL
MARCH 5

When I was little, my aunt had an accident and was hospitalized. She had fallen, broken her leg, and also injured her eye. The next time I saw her, I was terrified and wouldn't go anywhere near her. She came into the house hobbling on crutches, wearing an eye patch, with purple and red bruises on her face. That person didn't look like my aunt at all! I thought she was some kind of alien or monster.

Fortunately, my aunt sat down next to me and told me that she was still her, underneath all those bruises, the eyepatch, the crutches, and the leg cast. She understood why I was scared, but assured me, "I'm still me! And I love you!" I felt so much better, and I gave her a hug.

What an analogy for what happens to us in life! We get banged up, but we have to remember our Truth. Underneath all the eyepatches, the bruises, the unwanted conditions, and the difficult circumstances we might not like, the Truth of who and what we are is always there. Each one of us is a child of God. Perfect, whole, and complete in our divinity. This is true for you, and it is true for everyone.

Act

When you see people in your life "banged up" by human conditions, remember the Truth of who they are.

GRACE
MARCH 6

Do you work well under pressure? Putting pressure on yourself with regard to your mental, metaphysical, and spiritual activity is counterintuitive. Effort defeats itself. You can't *force* your mind to think rightly. We want so badly to manifest the life we desire, but the "wanting" ends up creating tension within us. It is like trying to force and rush the Creative Process.

You have the opportunity to give yourself some grace when navigating new spiritual principles and practices. Can you approach spirituality from a relaxed state of mind and be gentle with yourself? Can you trust in the flow of Life?

Affirm

I let Divine Love and grace surround my spiritual journey.

AFFIRMATIONS FOR TODAY:
MARCH 7

Affirm

I have the power to create the life I desire.
I live in harmony with the Infinite Intelligence of the Universe.
I am open and ready to receive my good.
The Peace of God is at the center of my being.
I choose the things that bring me joy.
I allow myself the grace of self-care.
I trust the Universe fully!
It is done unto me as I believe.
I am aware of my thoughts and how powerful they are.
All is well in my life.

HONOR ALL PATHS
MARCH 8

As a minister, I often begin funeral services by saying, "Please join me, and pray to the God of your understanding." I do this because the people in the audience may be of all different faiths and religions. They may have different understandings of God. They may be operating at different levels or states of consciousness, on very different divine seeking paths. All the levels, all the paths, all the different understandings are leading to the same God. It is all the same universal power.

Imagine if we gave each other grace and honored all our unique paths and understanding, every hour, every moment of every day? Nothing bad happens to us when we graciously allow someone else to follow the path that works for them. On the contrary, something good happens: the oneness of humanity is realized.

Affirm

I honor all paths to the One Universal God.

ALGORITHM OF ATTENTION
MARCH 9

The Law of Attraction teaches that what we focus on expands, magnifies, and grows. Energy flows where our attention goes. It is Spiritual Law that our thoughts and attention create our reality. Social media algorithms are a great example of how this principle works. If you get sucked into watching videos that are dramatic, scary, or negative, and you continue watching that kind of content, the social media app will continue to show you more of that content. You create what is before you because you are focused on that kind of material. That is what the algorithm is intended to do.

It's challenging, but we can be aware of our attention and our thoughts and how they translate to creating our life experience. When we notice our social media apps being flooded with content we don't want to see, we can clean it up by consciously ignoring things we don't want and deliberately focusing more on what we do want to see. We can even go out of our way to search for, watch, and enjoy the content we do want to see. Everything before us is there because we allow it to be.

Affirm

Today, I am mindful of my focus, thoughts, and attention.
I am in charge of my life experience!

YOU ARE THE BENEFICIARY
MARCH 10

The word *beneficiary* calls to mind a situation where a person receives benefits, funds, or property from a life insurance policy or a last will and testament. This person receives the things freely, through no action of their own. This is our role in the grand scheme of life—that of a beneficiary. The Infinite Intelligence of God gives to us the good that surrounds us, comes to us, and flows through us. Our good is our gift, and it is freely given.

There is only one thing we need to do to participate in this divine scenario. We need to receive it. It is up to us whether we want to accept the abundance available to us. When we look to nature and see that the birds do not struggle to meet their needs, and the flowers don't labor at displaying their beauty, we can also trust in knowing that our own health, prosperity, love, and peace are also all in good supply.

Affirm

I am the beneficiary of all life, simply because I exist.
My good is at hand.

SELF-INQUIRY QUESTIONS
MARCH 11

Self-inquiry helps you question and understand your thoughts, beliefs, emotions, and behavior. It takes great self-awareness and maturity to honestly and openly examine your inner self, but when you do, rest assured, this practice can lead to emotional, spiritual, and physical well-being. The process doesn't need to be complicated. Take these questions to meditation, prayer, contemplative thought, or your journal. The only requirement is your willingness to be open and honest, without judgment.

Ask

Who am I?
What do I believe about myself and the world?
What patterns do I see play out in my life?
What would I do if I believed I could not fail?
What inner gifts do I long to share with the world?
What, if anything, is holding me back from having the life I desire?

LIFE IS THERE
MARCH 12

An old story goes that an Egyptian mummy was found buried holding seeds in its hand. The seeds had been dormant for centuries. When the seeds were planted, they still grew! The life principle within the seeds was there, just waiting for the right conditions so they could grow.

Isn't that strange to think about? The hands that held the seeds were dead! This is a great analogy for the Divine Truth that lies within the mind, body, and soul for each of us individually. That seed—that spark of life—is always there, just waiting for us to put our awareness on it. We have the choice to pay attention to that Truth, to bring it to life, and cultivate it. Or we can ignore it, having a low, "dead" consciousness.

Ask

What does this idea bring to life in me?
What is waiting to be born and made manifest from my conscious awareness?

YOU ARE A CHANNEL
MARCH 13

How often during the day do you shift your awareness to the God-Presence? Do you do this when you are working at your job, whatever business that might be? Is the One Presence of the Divine present in your finances and your business affairs? How could it not be? Are you not a channel for God's great good, expressing in, through, and as your work, your creativity, your prosperity, and life experience? Can you actively remember throughout your day that the God-Presence is with you, leading you, guiding you? Consider this your reminder: you are a channel for the Divine.

Affirm

God's work is my work.
God's ideas are my ideas, and they are very good.

SPIRITUAL DEVELOPMENT
MARCH 14

What comes to mind when you hear the words *spiritual development*? What is developing? Is there an endpoint to this development? Spiritual development isn't necessarily something to be accomplished or completed, but rather, an ongoing attitude and way of life. Perhaps spiritual development is more like deciding what general direction your life will flow, moving in alignment and toward the God-Source. It is an ongoing process, something to be learned, studied, and cultivated, but perhaps never finished. There is no challenge to this, no hard work, no difficulty to overcome.

Spiritual development is the natural, graceful unfolding of your soul awareness. We are, all of us, on a spiritual journey of unfoldment.

Ask

What does my spiritual development journey look like today?

GOD IS HERE
MARCH 15

The next time you are stressed out or having a bad day, take a moment to slow down, pause, and breathe. When we pause to remember that God is everywhere, always, in all ways, it means that even during our most stressful, chaotic days, God is here. You can safely trust and believe in the Omnipresence of God. It is within you in every moment.

For instance, whenever and wherever you are you reading these words, it is "right now" for you. God is here. Right now. Whether it's a great day you're experiencing or the worst day of your life. There is stability and security in shifting your awareness to this Truth.

Act

Let go of your fear. Let go of your joy.
Let go of your stress. Let go of your bliss.
Let go of your pain. Let go of your love.
Let go of your story. Let go of all spiritual effort.

What is left?
The neutral Omnipresence of the Divine.
Everything is okay. God is here.

THANKS FOR THE DIFFICULTY
MARCH 16

We know we can consciously give thanks for all our good, but that is just one way to practice gratitude. Another way is to be grateful for the bad things that happen to us. That may sound crazy, but consider these examples:

A diagnosis of a serious illness is terrifying, but maybe that diagnosis is the reason you change your habits and take better care of your body. You can have gratitude for that health warning that your body gave you.

Maybe an abusive relationship helped you learn to respect and value yourself. It might have pushed you to consider the healthy relationship that you deserve.

You could have gratitude for the years spent at a miserable job because it made you uncomfortable and gave you clarity about what you didn't want to experience.

Difficult moments motivate us to do better, think better, believe better, and live more in alignment with our Truth.

Ask

Can I look back over the negative, unfortunate things I have experienced in my life from the perspective of gratitude?

WISDOM WITHIN
MARCH 17

Human beings love to have things figured out. We like to know what we're doing. We like to be happy, prosperous, and successful. Where is the love and grace for those of us who don't have things figured out, who don't know what we're doing, and who don't feel successful at this moment?

We are all human, and there is always an opportunity to give ourselves some grace. The truth is, *we* may not know what we're doing, but the Spirit within us does know. That's what faith is about. It is knowing deep down that we don't have to have everything figured out. Spirit within you knows exactly what is happening and exactly what you need to do. You can trust in that, and you can trust in your ability to receive the guidance you need. It makes a big difference when you shift your consciousness to this kind of faith and belief. Stand a little straighter. Walk a little taller. The Wisdom of God is within you.

Affirm

I have access to all the wisdom, guidance, and support I could ever need.

HEARTBEAT EXERCISE
MARCH 18

Have you ever read about or seen news footage of a tragic world event that deeply upset you to your core? You can feel the tension and discomfort in your body, and your heart pounds. Other people are also responding in this way, feeling their heart beating in their chest. A beating heart is something all people have in common. It's a great reminder of our oneness. What if our awareness of everyone's hearts beating together in harmony could lift the consciousness of people and positively change the world? We are all connected in the One Source of all life. Our oneness and unity are real. We feel pain when we see people hurt and suffering because we are one.

Act

When you feel upset, unsure how to process your pain, and unsure how to help humanity, focus on your heartbeat.

Affirm

At the center of my being, my heart is an instrument of peace, love, and healing.

HOW ARE YOU?
MARCH 19

Did you know it is almost impossible to say something about yourself without using the words: "I am?" When asked, "How are you?" you respond, "I am fine," or "I am sick," or "I am… whatever." Scripture tells us that *I AM* is the name of God, so when we use these words in our everyday language to speak about ourselves, we are quite literally invoking the name of God when we do it (Exod. 3:14).

If you do this negatively, and say things like, "I am sick," or "I am poor," or "I am lonely," it doesn't make any sense from a spiritual perspective. The Divine can't be any of those things. We want what follows our I AM to be in alignment with our true self, our divine nature. We want to be speaking of our highest good, our best life. Remember this when you say, "I am… anything!"

Ask

What positive Divine Truth can I affirm after my I AM?

THE CREATIVE PROCESS: SPRING
MARCH 20

As winter fades, the snow begins to melt. The sun shines, and signs of spring start to appear. We see budding trees, blooming flowers, and sprouting seeds. Such evidence of life is beautiful and exciting! Spring shows us the demonstration and the manifestation of winter's silent work. The world knows that what takes place in the darkness of winter can be trusted. There is no need to dig up the bulbs we buried last fall. Buried in that cold, dormant soil, a new experience awaits us every year. Every time, without fail. We celebrate when we see the results. The work is done!

So it is with our spiritual work—the Creative Process. The blossoms of spring acknowledge that creation is real. Whatever springs forth comes from the silent work—our prayers, our affirmations, our thoughts. We can trust that we will see the proof of our hard work.

Affirm

Manifestations come.
The desires and outcomes I wish to see spring forth!

DON'T BE A LOOKY-LOO
MARCH 21

There is a human phenomenon called the "looky-loo," where a person goes somewhere to look at something (such as the scene of an accident or law enforcement incident) and behaves like an intrusively curious onlooker. A "looky-loo" is often nosy about things that aren't their business and ends up being in the way. The person often regrets seeing the gory details of the scene they came upon.

We are always in control of what we look at, pay attention to, seek out, immerse ourselves in, and ingest. Be careful with your attention. When we keep our attention focused on divine spiritual principle, our intention is naturally more in alignment with Source. It is important to practice this, even when we are tempted to look at something we shouldn't. Use today's affirmation as a mantra.

Affirm

My attention is my intention.

HEALING WORK
MARCH 22

No one wants to receive a concerning health diagnosis from a doctor about a condition, illness, or disease. Medical practitioners treat us with therapies, treatments, and medication, but what can we do to actively participate in our own healing process?

Sometimes, we have to open ourselves to the idea that there could be unprocessed emotions, past trauma, false beliefs, and negative thoughts impacting and influencing our expression of health. Our mind, body, and spirit are all connected. Just opening yourself up to ideas like this can shift your consciousness and change your health experience. Here are some deep questions to journal about and consider.

Ask

Am I holding on to emotions from the past?
How am I thinking about my body?
How am I speaking about my health to others?
Am I willing to change my thought patterns?

Act

If necessary, seek professional help from a spiritual practitioner, therapist, or counselor to help you identify emotional areas of concern.

FORGIVEN
MARCH 23

Many religions and faith traditions are based on concepts of condemnation, repentance, sin, and moral judgment. Many insist that God forgives us for any mistake we could possibly make, so long as we submit to and follow the instructions of that particular religious teaching and church leadership. This mixes the idea of controlling human behavior with the idea of God's unconditional and automatic forgiveness and love, which is troubling. God is not interested in controlling behavior.

A radically different way to think is to consider that perhaps God does not forgive because God does not condemn in the first place. When you recognize your unity and oneness with the Universal God, you realize there is nothing you could possibly do to need forgiveness. You are an expression of the Divine, perfect, whole, and complete. You have simply forgotten your unity and oneness with God. You cannot be separated from the Divine because you *are* divine.

Affirm

Today, I remember my unity and oneness with God.
There is nothing for which I need to be forgiven.

WORK IT
MARCH 24

New Thought minister and teacher, Johnnie Coleman, published a book titled, *It Works If You Work It*, which reminds us to step up our spiritual practice game—the "work" we do to maintain connection with our true divine self. Spiritual practice can look like different things for different people. Reading spiritual books is a spiritual practice (you're doing it right now). Other spiritual practices include meditation, prayer, journaling, exploring nature, chanting, sound baths, attending spiritual services, yoga, gratitude, sitting in silence, writing affirmations, etc. Spiritual practice is our "work that works when we work it" because it brings us closer to and more in alignment with the Divine. It not only improves our life experience, it IS our life experience.

Ask

What is the daily work I do to remember my Truth?

SPIRITUAL RESET
MARCH 25

I recently experienced a frustrating day. I was irritated with the behavior of a few people in my family. Then I had to call customer service for a problem I was having with a company, and that call was very frustrating. Then I got so worked up and irritated that I became frustrated with myself! I was feeling full of doubt and irritation. It was not a good day. I needed a spiritual reset.

Fortunately, I remembered that deep within me, at the center of my being, is that which is never frustrated, troubled, or scared. This is true for you as well. The next time you experience a conflict and have feelings of frustration, try this.

Act

Feel the feelings.
Express them in some way (speak it, write it, scream it into a pillow).
Stop, breathe deeply, and be still.
Mentally go to the spiritual Truth of your divine nature.

Affirm

Love and peace are within me in this moment.
My awareness of this is the key.

WHAT ARE YOU PLANTING?
MARCH 26

Anyone who has ever planted a backyard garden knows that when you plant corn, you get corn. A simple landscaping lesson tells you that when you plant the cutting of a rose bush, you get a rose bush. Galatians 6:7 tells us we reap what we sow. This is natural law; you harvest what you plant. What we might not realize is, this natural law applies to everything.

Kindness and compassion cultivate kindness and compassion. Anger and fighting result in more anger and more fighting. We are creating our life experiences with the thought seeds we plant in our minds. What are you planting? What are you seeing because of your planted thoughts? What are you envisioning, imagining, visualizing, thinking about, and expecting?

Act

If you don't like the harvest, plant something new!

ABOUT SAFETY...
MARCH 27

There are apps and websites that can tell you about all the crime that happens in your neighborhood. Even though we might think our neighborhood is completely safe, the app might show you that it isn't. You see every little altercation and police report, every incident that takes place.

Why would you want to change the way you think about your neighborhood and what you believe about your safety? Hearing about those little incidents influences your thoughts. When we think we are safe, that is often what is reflected in our experience. When we think we are in danger, the Universe will move to make it so you are indeed in danger. Remember, where your attention flows, energy goes.

Affirm

My thoughts create my world. I am safe.

PRAYER SIMPLIFIED
MARCH 28

What is prayer? It is so much more than the time we might spend in church with our hands folded and eyes closed. From a New Thought perspective, prayer is simply the habit and art of right thinking. When we become so conscious of the Presence of God within us that we naturally draw to us all the things that are fundamental for a good, abundant life—*that is prayer*. It is simple. Prayer is an awareness of your everyday thinking, speaking, and way of being. Be clear. Be mindful. Be present to your Truth.

Affirm

I am one with the Presence of God.
I trust that all is well.
This is my prayer.

BREATH OF LIFE
MARCH 29

Right now, in this present moment, check your jaw and see if you are holding tension there. If you are, let it go. Then check your shoulders. Roll them back a little bit. See if you can pull your shoulders farther away from your ears and just relax them. Take a long breath in for at least four seconds, and hold it at the top, and then release it for longer than four seconds—at least five or six seconds. That is it. That is the reading. That is the exercise. Just breathe. Just hold. Just exhale. Just relax.

You are being breathed by Spirit. This is truly breathing—being aware of this Truth. This is life. As you keep breathing, meditate on this.

Affirm

I am the breath of life.
Right now, I am aware that I am being breathed.

ACT ACCORDINGLY
MARCH 30

You are Divine. Act accordingly.
What does this mean to you?
Are you more God-like than you realize?
More peaceful? More loving?
Spiritually, you are perfect.
Is this how you express yourself in your daily life?
How can thinking about these ideas influence your life experience?

Affirm

*Today, I am aware of my divinity.
I am perfect just because I exist.*

INFINITE POSSIBILITIES
MARCH 31

What if that thing you are really worried, stressed, or scared about (the thing that is consuming your thoughts), what if it works out for your highest good? What if the thing you are worried about ends up working out better than you could possibly imagine? Why couldn't it?

We live in a field of infinite possibilities. There is a scenario where whatever the thing is that concerns you has a positive outcome. If every possible scenario exists in an invisible quantum field, then there must be an option you just haven't thought of yet, something you don't even know about—some solution to your challenge.

You can just as easily spend your time thinking about something good happening. Spend your time doing that. This is the easiest way to improve your life conditions, and it's free. All it takes is your conscious effort to change the way you think about something. Worry is misusing Spiritual Law, thinking about the outcome we don't want to experience. Instead, use your thought and imagination for good!

Affirm

I expect and anticipate the best-case scenario.

APRIL

GOD > PROBLEMS
APRIL 1

God is greater than any problem, situation, circumstance, or experience you could possibly encounter.

Act

Put your faith in that.
Think about that.
Talk about that.
Meditate on that.

Affirm

Today, I choose to put my faith in the Great Spirit of the Divine that exists within me, instead of putting my faith in my problems.

TRUE GIFTS
APRIL 2

When we give a gift to someone, we cover it in wrapping paper and put bows on top, or we put it in a gift bag. We do that so the person receiving the gift can't tell what it is—so the gift is a surprise. Have you ever considered that you are gift-wrapped?

God has packaged you in a lovely human body. Each of us is decorated differently, all different shapes and sizes, but the prize inside us all is the same divine essence as God. Our true task in life is to unwrap and understand our true gift—the gift of our divine nature.

Ask

Why am I here?
What is my true gift to humanity—my true divine expression?

THE NEXT THOUGHT
APRIL 3

"Your life can change as quickly as your next thought."

What does this mean to you? The truth is, no matter what is happening in your life, no matter what tragedies, troubles, problems, or traumas, you can always think a new thought that contradicts any negative experience. Consider these tips:

Feeling pain? *Think about what brings you pleasure.*
Feeling anger? *Think about something peaceful.*
Feeling hate? *Think about someone or something you love.*
Feeling depressed? *Think about what brings you joy.*
Feeling sick? *Think about what is healthy in your body.*
Feeling poor? *Think about gratitude.*

Ask

What if my next thought could change the trajectory of my life experience?

YOU DESERVE IT
APRIL 4

Nothing outside you has the power to withhold your good. Limitation takes place in our consciousness, not in our circumstances. In other words, if there is something that you want to have, do, or be, and you are feeling like you can't have it, do it, or be it, that's *not* true. That is limited thinking. We are the only ones who can block what's available to us and what we believe is possible for our lives.

Our own consciousness creates our life. Our experience and our conditions are a reflection of our consciousness. The idea that, "Only you can deprive yourself of anything," does not come from a place of blame. It comes from a place of great opportunity and responsibility. You are worthy of your good. You deserve it all.

Ask

Am I depriving myself of something I deserve with limited thinking?

LIT FROM WITHIN
APRIL 5

How often do you stop to affirm good things for your body? Take a moment now to consider the miraculous intelligence of your physical body. Can you envision your perfect health? What does it look like from the inside? Mentally go through your body, from the top of your head to the bottom of your feet. Think about, visualize, and imagine organs, body systems, and body parts fully illumined and lit with the Divine Light of health.

Go slowly, and think about the following: your brain, eyes, ears, nose, mouth, teeth, throat, thyroid, and esophagus. Move on to your shoulders, elbows, hands, heart, lungs, stomach, liver, gall bladder, spleen, pancreas, kidneys, sex organs, intestines, bladder, and rectum. Consider your pelvis, hips, knees, ankles, feet, and toes. Also, remember your joints, muscles, ligaments, glands, bones, blood, cells, and skin.

Acknowledge that your body is expressing as Infinite Intelligence, and you radiate Divine Wholeness. Every cell in your body knows exactly what to do for optimum health.

Affirm

I am healthy, whole, and complete.
From my head to my toes, I am filled with Divine Light.

PERFECT PATTERNS
APRIL 6

God's perfection is in all things—all life, and that includes you. There is a pattern to the perfection, a pattern that we can invite into our awareness and recognize. We see perfect patterns of spiritual perfection in the universe everywhere, from the planets rotating in perfect orbit to how plants and trees grow from tiny seeds and the way animals instinctively know how to survive. Our human bodies are no different. Divine life force energy is at the core of our being. We can decide at any given moment to seek out and recognize God's perfect pattern in humanity, in ourselves, and in all people.

Affirm

God's perfect divine pattern is everywhere. Today, I choose to look for it.

JOURNALING FOR MANIFESTATION
APRIL 7

Journaling is a spiritual practice that can be used to manifest your desires. For example, if you are wanting to manifest a new home, write from the perspective that you have already found this home, can easily afford it, and are living comfortably in it. Write and describe this perfect home. The details aren't as important as invoking how you will feel once you have the experience of living in it. Is it comfortable? Cozy? What is the lighting like? Is it warm and inviting? What is it about this home that makes you so happy? How does it feel to be able to afford this dream home?

Journaling about our good and the good we expect to receive helps us manifest the life we desire!

Ask

What can I journal about and manifest today?

THIS TEMPORARY EXPRESSION
APRIL 8

It is easy to forget that our natural state, our Divine Truth, is that we are much more than a body. We are souls, and the soul has no use for a body. This certainly puts death in a different perspective! Our time as humans is simply one expression of our ongoing life experience. When that time ends, the body is left behind, and we return to our natural state. This is what is meant when most, if not all, religions teach that life is eternal. Think about this the next time you find yourself distracted by your human body problems. Whatever it is, and however you label it, it is temporary, and it is not your true state of being.

Affirm

My true state is without a body at all. I am a soul.

PERFECT GOODNESS
APRIL 9

Even though we may see suffering, limitation, and doubt all around us, we can, at any moment, shift our attention to the perfect goodness of God that is within each one of us. Let us do this now with an Affirmative Prayer. Receive these words for yourself.

Pray

I know there is only One Power, One Source, One Life, and it is God's Life. This Perfect Life is my life now. It is gifted to me because I am a child of God. I know beyond a doubt that a spark of divinity lies within me. No matter how often I forget, it is still there, no matter how often I am told I am unworthy, I can choose in any moment to circle back to the Truth. I choose this moment right now, to be still and remember—to put my awareness on my oneness with the Divine.

I graciously accept the unconditional Love of Spirit. I let it fill my being so much that it spills forth out of me to touch others. I am so grateful for the goodness of God and all the ways it expresses in me, through me, and as me. There is great good in the world, and from this moment on, I choose to believe it, see it, and experience it.

And So It Is. Amen

TRUST IN SOLUTIONS
APRIL 10

Have you ever seen a toddler get frustrated when they don't know how to do something, or they have a problem they can't solve? In moments like this, toddlers are famous for throwing tantrums. Adults do the same thing to varying degrees. We might become angry and frustrated when we can't figure out a problem. While feeling and expressing our emotions can be perfectly healthy, anger, frustration, and sadness are not the ones we like to spend a lot of time on. And we don't have to. Solutions are available to us. Spirit operates in solutions, not problems, and Spirit is within you.

The truth is that guidance comes to the person who expects it. If you are experiencing a problem, remember that the One Mind of Spirit that knows all and is all is within you. You have access to It. So, if you don't know the answer, something within you does know. You can relax and trust that the answer will be revealed to you. As you prepare to fall asleep tonight, shift your awareness to this Truth.

Affirm

Spirit within me operates in solutions,
and I expect to receive these solutions.
Divine answers are within me!

THE DEADLINE PRAYER
APRIL 11

Have you ever had a deadline you had to meet, to finish your work, or accomplish something specific? Deadlines can fill you with anxiety and make you feel stressed. The next time you are worried about a deadline, affirm the Truth of this Spiritual Mind Treatment:

Pray

There is only One Power, One Presence, One Life—it is God's Life, and it is Perfect. That Life is my life now. God's Life is Divine Intelligence, Wisdom, and Harmony. There is no such thing as time in Spirit. Time is a human construct. There are no limits, restrictions, or deadlines. All is well in Spirit. I am one with this One Power of God—one with Divine Intelligence. All the Wisdom, Knowledge, and Creativity that I could possibly want or need is available to me in this moment. My mind is part of the One Mind of Spirit. I have access to everything I need. There is no need for stress, so right now in this moment, I release and let go of all sense of panic, anxiety, and fear.

I put my faith and trust in the Truth that Wisdom, Intelligence, and Creativity are mine. This work is already done. God's ideas are my ideas. I am open to the perfect flow of ideas to me and through me. I say yes to being an expression of God's great ideas. This is a natural, easy process that is unfolding. I give great thanks for this, for everything that God is, and for the opportunity to express as it all. I am grateful for the Creative Process and my part in it. This is the way Life works! There is nothing left to do but release this treatment into the action of the Law, fully anticipating and expecting its fulfillment, trusting that all is well.

And So It Is.

OVERTHINK THE GOOD STUFF
APRIL 12

The dictionary defines overthinking as: *"thinking about something too much or for too long."* But this definition fails to acknowledge that overthinking is almost always negative. Have you ever heard of an entrepreneur overthinking about her business making too much money? How about a man overthinking all the excellent medical test results he will receive at his next doctor visit? How about the woman who worries her new relationship is going to go too well? We are never overwhelmed by positive possible scenarios—we don't overthink the good stuff!

So often, we fall into negative overthinking accidentally, without realizing we are doing it. On the contrary, we never fall into positive thoughts accidentally. We have to make a conscious effort and move into positive thoughts purposely. That is okay! We can recognize our overthinking, our negative thought patterns, and move into a new positive thought pattern.

Affirm

I choose positive patterns of thought and let them run wild in my mind!

CHILDHOOD BELIEFS
APRIL 13

Sometimes the ideas we were taught as children no longer resonate with us when we are grown. Even worse, sometimes we realize that the concepts we learned when we were young are detrimental to our well-being as adults. For instance, if you were told as a child that your family was poor and you had parents who insisted there was never enough money, you might grow up and have false beliefs about money and abundance. You might have a horrible attitude about your ability to work, be prosperous, and experience the financial success you deserve. You might believe that being poor is your lot in life. It is important to remember that beliefs can always be changed.

Regardless of any false ideas you learned as a child, you are an adult now. You are responsible for your own attitudes and beliefs. You get to choose how to think and what you want to believe.

Ask

Do I have childhood beliefs that need adjusting?

KEEP LISTENING
APRIL 14

I once attended a private concert where a husband and wife played dueling harps. It was a small, intimate venue, with less than fifty people in attendance. Even though the harp is a string instrument that creates soft, gentle sounds, the concert was quite moving and powerful. When the strings are plucked (unless someone puts their hand against the string to stop it from vibrating), the sound continues to reverberate out. That means you are still hearing the previous note, even when the musician moves on to pluck another string to create the next note. The music echoed in the tiny venue, which made the concert feel mystical and magical.

The experience reminded me of the energy bar chime that I use during my meditation practice. I strike the chime, and the sound reverberates for several seconds, long after I hit it. That is my opportunity to listen, to choose to be calm and still. When we choose to keep listening in that moment, while an instrument's reverberation lingers, it is our chance to recognize our happiness and peace.

Ask

*Where in my life can I listen more deeply
and practice this kind of stillness and mindfulness?*

MOVE YOUR FEET
APRIL 15

We know it is wise to change and update our passwords from time to time. Why do we do this? We don't typically walk around having the thought or expectation that our accounts and passwords will be hacked. We don't think someone is out there actively trying to access our information. We wouldn't put our faith in such negative, fearful thoughts. We would put our faith in the opposite, knowing that we are safe, protected, and secure.

But, at the same time, we can be proactive and protect ourselves by regularly changing our passwords. In New Thought circles and centers, there is a common saying: "Treat, then move your feet," which means pray a Spiritual Mind Treatment or Affirmative Prayer (have faith), and then move your feet. Take some action in the direction of that faith. This movement is like the action of changing your passwords. We can do things to aid Spirit's demonstration of our security, while stepping out in faith with the confident assurance that our manifest desire is unfolding.

Affirm

Today, I take any action necessary to move in the direction of my faith.

IT IS ALREADY HERE
APRIL 16

We can spend a lot of time searching for God in the midst of our busy lives. We try to add the Divine to our existence, perhaps by reading about it, talking about it with others, or listening to others talk about it. There is a difference between actively trying to find God and coming to the realization that God is already here. You do not need to *find* anything. You need only recognize that the God-Presence is already here. It is the very essence of your being.

This concept is similar to the work of archaeology. Archaeologists do not go looking for things to put in the earth. They dig up what is already there, things that have been buried deep underground for centuries. They gently uncover what is there, meticulously brushing away the dirt, sand, mud—anything that is unlike the artifact they are discovering, anything that is in the way of revealing what is right there. This is our endeavor as human beings—to uncover what is already there within each one of us.

Act

*Any outward search of the Divine must end
with the ultimate discovery of God at the center of your being.
Go within.*

POSSIBILITY QUESTIONS
APRIL 17

Jesus represents man's great potential. He understood his unity with the Divine more than anyone who ever lived. Because of that, he was able to accomplish great things, including many miracles. His teaching demonstrates to humanity that when we understand our individual unity with God, all things are possible. Consider this an opportunity to stop and ask yourself these questions:

Ask

What is possible for my life?
What is possible for my abundance?
What is possible for my relationships?
What is possible for my creativity?
What is possible for my career?
What possibilities can I experience
because of my unity with the Divine?

TITHE FOR PROSPERITY
APRIL 18

Tithing is a commitment of giving, usually to a religious organization and most often in the form of an ongoing monetary donation. But tithing can be understood more broadly, as a covenant between you and the Divine, a universal tool that can be used to increase your awareness of abundance and prosperity. There are so many ways to generously give of yourself. You can tithe of your time, talent, and treasure in order to more wholly experience the fullness of life that comes directly from Source.

Giving of your time might look like committing to regularly attending spiritual services. It could also look like taking spiritual development classes or committing to a regular spiritual practice like meditation. Give your time to God.

Giving of your talent might look like volunteering for your spiritual center or other nonprofit organization. It could be choosing to share your skills with your friends and neighbors to serve your community. Give your talent to humanity.

Giving of your treasure might look like committing to donate a small percentage of your income and wealth to your church organization, another nonprofit, or anyone who is in need of financial resources. Give your money so it serves the world.

Giving in these ways shifts our consciousness about prosperity, opening us up to a more abundant life.

Affirm

*I am willing to give of my time, talent,
and treasure in order to raise my consciousness regarding prosperity.*

BELIEF CHECK
APRIL 19

Get into the habit of examining your beliefs. This is an observational exercise that can spark deep spiritual insight. Remember, long-held beliefs might not be true. False beliefs can always be changed. Read through the following statements. If any of them represent a belief you hold, stop and ask yourself: Is this really true?

Marriage is a struggle.
Rich people are greedy.
My allergies act up every spring.
Once you retire, there is no more purpose in your life.
You get one chance to have a soulmate.
Poor people are lazy.
Every time I fly on a plane, I get sick.
It's impossible to run a successful small business these days.
Men eventually abandon women.
Single mothers must struggle to survive financially.
When you hit a certain age, your body falls apart.
The purpose of a job is to pay the bills.
Women are gold diggers.
It's impossible to save money these days.
For me, love doesn't last.
I'm always underappreciated at work.

Ask

What other beliefs can I examine and question?

DIVINE TIMING
APRIL 20

Do you think you have good timing? It's an interesting concept, the idea that we can have something happen at the most opportune moment, that we can be in the right place at the right time for a favorable experience or outcome. But timing is a human construct. Time itself is a human invention; there is no time in Spirit.

Consider the phrase: "Divine Timing." Divine Timing is a spiritual belief that everything already happens at the exact perfect moment. We can tune into Divine Timing by paying attention to our intuition, noticing synchronicities, and looking for signs that guide us through life. This is living and trusting in Divine Flow.

Affirm

Whatever I need is revealed to me at exactly the right time.
I live in Divine Flow.

THREE POINT BACK
APRIL 21

When we judge another person, an image comes to mind of pointing your finger at someone aggressively. Put your hand in that position now, making your index finger point outward and away from you. Where are your other three fingers pointing, the ones under your thumb? They point back toward you. This is a great illustration of the way consciousness works.

Conditions in our life, people we encounter, situations we experience are always an out picturing of our consciousness. When we see something we don't like, some behavior that frustrates us, or a quality we are quick to judge or condemn, we must ask ourselves where in our own life do we see the same behavior or quality? The next time you want to judge, label, or react, think about those other three fingers.

Ask

Why does this behavior bother me?
Do I also exhibit this quality?
Is there something within me that is like this outer circumstance that I see?
Have I ever behaved similarly?
What in my consciousness is being reflected here?
What can I learn from this situation?

YOU GET TO
APRIL 22

Gratitude is a spiritual principle that draws our good to us, giving us more things to be grateful for. It is, of course, a good idea to be thankful for what we have, but gratitude is also a great strategy to use when we have to do something that we don't want to do. For instance, consider something like exercise. We all know we should exercise to keep our bodies healthy. It is good to be active, but we can also feel lazy. Sometimes we just don't want to work out. When we shift our thought to a place of gratitude—the fact that we have a body that we can move, it makes doing the thing we don't want to do a little bit easier by changing our perspective.

Perhaps you can think of someone you might know who is disabled and confined to a wheelchair. That person is unable to walk, exercise, or move their body. When you are feeling lazy and are grumbling because you don't want to exercise, you can shift your thought and instead think, "I *get* to work out. I *get* to take a walk. I am able to use this body and exercise, and for that I am so grateful!" It shifts your thinking and makes the thing you don't really want to do more manageable.

Ask

What projects, activities, and commitments am I tasked with in my life that I can approach from a place of gratitude?

READY TO RECEIVE
APRIL 23

Think of something that you want to manifest or wish to draw into your life. Now, ask yourself, are you actively behaving and living as if you have already received it? Are you living from the end result that you wish to see? That is the mindset that puts Spiritual Law in motion and causes demonstrations of your good.

Additionally, we need to make room for our good before it can appear. Have you cleaned out the proverbial closet and gotten ready to receive the thing you are wanting to manifest? If the thing you want was delivered to you tomorrow morning, would you be prepared for it? Are you mentally and physically behaving as if the desired thing is already yours? You get what you want when you are ready to receive it. Are you ready?

Affirm

I choose to live as if I have already received.
I am ready to receive my good.

YOU ARE THE THINKER
APRIL 24

As minister and teacher Johnnie Coleman used to say, "I am the thinker that thinks the thought that makes the thing." Much like how Jesus knew it was not him, but the power within him that did the work, this idea reminds us that _we_ are not the power that creates anything. Spiritual Law, God, Universe, Source, whatever we want to call it, is doing the work. It is the power. We just use the power.

We think the thought that puts the Creative Process in motion. This is how powerful our thoughts are. This is how powerful you are. You are the thinker. You have no time for idle, negative thoughts. They produce things you don't want.

Affirm

I am always in charge of the thoughts I think.

CLEAN YOUR GLASSES
APRIL 25

Recently, I was reading something to my husband while wearing my reading glasses. He pointed out that my glasses were very dirty. I told him it was fine, I could still see. He said, "Imagine how clear things will be if you cleaned them." This is a great spiritual metaphor. Taking the time to clean our glasses is work, but the results help us see better and make our lives better!

Spiritual practice is the work we do to bring clarity to our lives. Whether through meditation, prayer, attending a religious service, journaling, walking in nature, reading a spiritual book like this one, or something else, we can make the effort to "clean up" our thinking and live more in alignment with Source.

Affirm

Spiritual practice brings me clarity.

ARE YOU HAVING ANY FUN?
APRIL 26

A dancing bobblehead Jesus sits on my kitchen windowsill. This is the third house of mine he has lived in. He's been with me for so long that sometimes, I forget he's there. Occasionally, when a person comes to my home for the first time, they notice him and say something like, "What in the world? Is that Jesus?" They laugh and can't believe I would have such a silly toy.

Spirituality need not be stuffy, boring, or humorless. Our spiritual life should be taken seriously, but never too seriously. Joy is a powerful, high-frequency attractor of good. Laughter lessens our stress, depression, and anxiety. Spiritual principles are meant to be played with and tested.

Act

Remember to have fun on your spiritual journey!

A PRAYER FOR PEACE
APRIL 27

Pray

What I know to be true is there is only One Power, One Source, One Life. It is God's Life, and it is Perfect. It is an expression of Peace, Love, and Harmony. That is our true nature; it is the nature of all life. I live, and move, and have my being in this One Power. I know this is true for all life, and that includes you. I know it is true for the leaders of countries in conflict and all the citizens of those countries. I pray for the realization of this peaceful Truth. I believe all things are possible, and I believe peace is possible.

I have the expectation and the anticipation that peace prevails. This is what I project and carry out into the world with my attitude, thoughts, and beliefs. I am so grateful for the Creative Process and for all the ways peace unfolds in this world. I give thanks for the peace I feel in my heart in this moment. I am grateful that we are all one, that our peaceful, divine nature is at the center of all of us.

And So It Is. Amen.

PRAY IMMEDIATELY
APRIL 28

Once, in a busy intersection, I was following the car in front of me too closely at five miles per hour. The person ahead of me hit their brakes, and I hit their car. I had my children with me, we were late for an appointment, and I could not afford any car repairs. My mood instantly shifted to anger, frustration, disappointment, and impending lack.

I had to wait for the light to change so we could move our vehicles out of the way and exchange information. In those few seconds, I prayed. I trusted that God was present. I was grateful no one was hurt. There was no reason to jump to the conclusion that this would be a difficult, costly, drawn-out problem. I believed in the possibility that there could be little to no damage. Before the accident, all was well in my mind. I remembered how it felt to know that all was well. This accident was nothing! When the light changed, I moved to the side of the road. Then something crazy happened.

Instead of pulling over, the other driver drove away! I had hit him, and he drove away. When I got out of my car, I was amazed to see no damage at all. A police officer friend explained that sometimes this happens, especially if the other driver is under the influence, guilty of a crime, or uninsured. They just leave the scene. There was nothing for me to report. I returned to an attitude of carefree assuredness and went on with my day like nothing ever happened. Was it my immediate prayer?

Affirm

Prayer works, and I remember to use it.

WE ARE SMALL
APRIL 29

Have you ever seen the Milky Way? Not just the regular stars you might see from your backyard, but a true glimpse of our galaxy? If you drive far away from city lights on a clear night, sometimes you can see how vast and incredible our galaxy is. You can lie on your back and see the stars of the Milky Way moving above you.

Only the stars aren't turning. It is the earth that is rotating. We humans think we are so big, but we are actually very small. We have so much happening in our lives with our fighting and our drama, our striving for success, and our go, go, go. Life is so much more than that. We are like tiny cogs in an infinitely intelligent, creative wheel.

Affirm

My soul is a tiny spark of starlight in the vast process of eternal Life.

IT'S FINE
APRIL 30

I once knew a young girl whose response to almost everything was, "It's fine!" Whether she was being asked to clean up her room, comb her hair, or study for a test at school, she would always respond, "It's fine!" Some perceived her as being lazy and not putting forth her best effort. As the child grew up into a beautiful adult woman, it became clear that "It's fine" was really her mantra for "All is well." It was part of her belief that all was well in her life. There was no reason to trouble her mind.

She didn't let the conditions and circumstances of the world or things that needed to get done bother her. This was a part of her belief system, knowing that it was fine, no matter what went on in her life. When she had this attitude, conditions in her life seemed to flourish. Good things fell into her lap unexpectedly. She lived in harmony and experienced more joy.

Ask

Where in my life can I stop and say, "It's fine," and see if situations in my life improve?

MAY

USE THE POWER FOR GOOD
MAY 1

Students of New Thought understand there is a power for good moving through the universe at all times. We use this power through the thoughts we think and the beliefs we hold in our subconscious mind. But what about people who don't know about this power? They also think thoughts and have beliefs. The truth is, we use the power whether or not we are aware of it and whether or not we are aware of the thoughts we think. God, Spirit, Universe, Source (whatever word you use for Spiritual Law) always responds to our thoughts.

If you are complaining about your life circumstances and conditions, giving negative thoughts your attention, Spirit responds, "Yes, I'm going to give you more of that. I'll give you more things to complain about." That's how Spiritual Law works. But once you understand this, you can start affirming good things for your life. Focusing on your thoughts and letting go of false beliefs is how the magic happens. It is how transformation begins.

Affirm

I can transform my life by changing my thoughts and beliefs!

TAKE THE DARE
MAY 2

To *dare* means to have courage and boldness. Even when used as a noun, *dare* means *a challenge posed to someone to test their courage and boldness*. Would you describe yourself as courageous and bold? Do you like to accept dares?

I dare you to think courageously and boldly about yourself today. I dare you to believe that the same qualities of love, power, and peace that were in the saints and masters, like Jesus, Buddha, Krishna, and Allah, are also in you. I dare you to believe that when you speak the powerful words, "I AM," declaring anything about yourself, you are invoking the name of God. I dare you to live, move, and have your being in the One Mind, One Life, One Consciousness of God. I dare you to live in this awareness fully, today, and every day.

Ask

Do I accept this dare?

WEIGHT OF THE WORLD
MAY 3

How do you handle tragic news? Current events? The details of war and conflict in the world? Famine? Mass murder? Innocent civilian death? Do you ignore these uncomfortable matters and choose not to watch the news at all? Do you connect with friends and loved ones for comfort? Do you rely on spiritual practice? What tips and tricks do you use for handling the weight of the world's problems?

While deep down we know and trust that we are united and one with all humanity, it can be deeply challenging to really feel this in our day-to-day lives. This entry doesn't come with a clear-cut answer for guidance. The purpose of it is to have you consider how you can best serve yourself and remember your Truth.

Ask

What can I do to actively, consciously shift my awareness to the oneness of humanity, despite what I am seeing around me?
What is mine to do in any given moment?
How can I best serve the spiritual evolution of humanity?

Act

Do what you need to do to protect your heart, mind, and spirit.
Read the things you need to read. Sit in the stillness.
Pray to the God of your understanding.
Affirm the Truth of your being.
Know the eternality of life.
Trust in the goodness of God.

INDIVIDUALIZED EXPRESSION
MAY 4

The Divine Science Statement of Being* (as it appears in the book *Divine Science: Its Principles and Practice*, compiled by Fannie B James and Malinda Cramer) reads:

> "God is all, both visible and invisible.
> One Presence, One Mind, One Power is all.
> This One that is all is perfect life, perfect love,
> and perfect substance.
> Man is the individualized expression of God and is ever one
> with this perfect life, perfect love, perfect substance."

Setting aside the outdated masculine language, take this statement into a time of reflection and meditation.

Affirm

*I am the individualized expression of God,
one with this perfect life, perfect love, perfect substance.*

---

* James, F. B., & Cramer, M. E. (1957). *Divine Science; Its Principles and Practice. compiled from Truth and Health, by Fannie B. James and Divine Science and Healing, by Malinda E. Cramer*. Textbook of Divine Science.

NO SEPARATION
MAY 5

There is nothing you can think, do, or be to separate yourself from God. It's not possible. You cannot be separate from God. There is One Life, that life is God's Life, that life is perfect, and you are an expression of that life. This should bring great comfort to a struggling human mind. No behavior, no mistake, no malicious act, no addiction, no angry word spoken, no failure, no suffering, *nothing* can separate you from God, not even your own insistence.

Affirm

I am one with the One Power, One Presence, One Life of God.

FIND WHAT IS HIDDEN
MAY 6

A Hindu legend says that thousands of years ago, men (and women) were all gods, but we abused our divinity. Brahma, the main Hindu god, took away man's divinity. He needed to hide it somewhere. The lower gods were giving suggestions for where he could hide man's divinity. One asked, "Why not put it deep in the earth?" Brahma said, "No, because I know man will dig and find it there."

Another suggested, "You could put it in the deepest ocean!" But Brahma said, "No, I know that man will figure out how to get into the water and find it." Yet another suggested, "Why don't you put it on the highest mountaintop?" Brahma said, "No, surely man will just climb up the mountain and get to it."

Then, Brahma decided that the best place to hide man's divinity was within himself, because man will never think to look there. The legend concludes that men and women have been searching and digging and diving and climbing all over the world to find the divinity that is within them. In so many ways, we are gods, and everything we could possibly need or want is hidden within us.

Affirm

When I realize what is within me, I transform my life.

WHEN THE NEWS IS UNSETTLING
MAY 7

Take a moment to pause and meditate.

Act

Allow your body to relax. Take a slow breath in and a long breath out. Do that again before you read the next sentence.

In this moment, there is nothing you need to do. Nothing to fix. Nothing you need to solve. Just rest.

As you breathe in a natural rhythm, remember that beyond all the headlines, the swirl of opinions, the fear that may grip you regarding the latest threat or tragedy, there is a deeper reality always present. It is an Infinite Good, a Universal Divine Presence. A Presence that is not shaken by any circumstance. Here and now, you are surrounded by, and immersed in, this Infinite Good.

You don't have to earn it. You don't have to create it—this Good just is. You are one with this Infinite Good, and this Good expresses itself as you.

On your next exhale, release the need to think about what needs to change in the world, who needs to do what, or how life should be.

Let yourself rest in something broader, something more universal. If God is Peace and you are one with God, then peace is present in you right now. Allow this peace to steady your nervous system and calm your thoughts. Breathe in peace. Breathe out anything that looks like chaos.

If God is Love and you are one with God, then love is here in this moment, in your awareness. This love is who and what you are at the core of your being. Breathe in love. Breathe out any fear. Love is more powerful than any false thought of fear.

Rest in this Truth.

BALANCING ACT
MAY 8

Fully grasping the dual nature of your life can be challenging. You are a human being experiencing life in a body, and you are also an eternal soul expressing as the Divine. Usually, we are focused on the first idea, wrapped up in what we experience with our senses and our limited human thinking. Occasionally, perhaps through spiritual practice like prayer, contemplation, or meditation, we get a glimpse of our expanded nature, our divinity, and our soul perspective. We may bounce back and forth with our awareness, from human life to our divine nature.

Can you live your life from both truths in a balanced way? This might be the ultimate goal—to experience human challenges, limitations, pain, etc., from the enlightened perspective that all is well on an eternal soul level.

Affirm

*Today, I choose to balance my awareness
between my human story and my soul perspective.*

THE PURPOSE OF TRANSFORMATION
MAY 9

Remodeling a home is a great opportunity to watch the transformation process. My husband and I once bought a house that we decided to transform with new carpet, flooring, baseboards, paint, interior doors, bathroom vanities, mirrors, toilets, etc. The projects were endless, and the messy chaos was everywhere. For several weeks after moving in, everything that would normally go in a pantry was in boxes on the floor of the kitchen because the pantry walls and shelves were not completed yet. For days, we stepped over piles of flooring material and tools that were always in the way. One day, we had to use the bathroom at the park down the street while our toilets were replaced. It was challenging to live that way, to say the least!

All these things were happening because the home was transforming and being changed for the better. Goals and intentions were set, and we were seeking a particular outcome: the finished product of our dream home. It was important for me to remember the purpose of the transformation. I held in my mind what the home would look like when it was all finished.

This applies to any kind of personal transformation we may undertake. If you are frustrated with the process, if it feels like it's taking too long, or if it seems challenging and chaotic, hold tight to your vision. Remember why you started in the first place.

Affirm

Transformation is a beautiful process;
I am focused on the outcome that I wish to see.

YOU'RE IN IT
MAY 10

A fish lived its whole life swimming, tirelessly searching, scanning, seeking the depths of the ocean at great length.

A second fish came along and asked, "What are you doing? What are you constantly looking for and seeking?"

The first fish said, "I have been told a great story that moves me. It is about a mystical, magical ocean. I long to find it, discover it for myself, and experience it fully. I know this ocean must be real. I believe it to be. It must be somewhere. I am doing everything I can to find it."

It's a silly story, but it beautifully illustrates the Omnipresence of God. Much like the fish in the story, *you're in it*—you are always surrounded by this One Presence of God. God does not hide Itself, and you do not need to seek It. You are in It, and It is in you.

Affirm

I am completely surrounded, supported, and loved by God.

FEAR VS. FAITH
MAY 11

Fear and faith seem like opposite concepts. Fear comes from the standpoint of "What if…?" It is followed by worry, complete with all the negative outcomes we can imagine. "What if…" calls to mind a frazzled, anxiety-ridden person who is biting their nails and living uncomfortably on the edge of their seat.

Faith comes from the standpoint of "Even if…!" Faith is followed by a peaceful, secure state of mind, no matter what outer circumstances lie before us. "Even if…" calls to mind a confident, serene person who knows that they are fully loved and supported by Spirit, no matter what happens in life.

Fear is rooted in nothingness. It is forgetting the Truth of who and what we are, mistakenly thinking we are alone.

Faith comes with a handy toolbox full of spiritual principles to study, spiritual practice to pursue, and a like-minded support system of friends, often found in a spiritual community. With faith, we can experience peace and assurance.

Affirm

Today, I choose faith over fear, knowing that with faith all things are possible.

IT IS WORTH IT
MAY 12

Sometimes, the pain of transformation and spiritual growth can feel uncomfortable, and no one likes to be uncomfortable. But much like how the pain of labor and delivery gives us the beauty of new life, transformational discomfort is also worth experiencing. Doing the spiritual work of diving deep, looking at our false beliefs, examining things we experienced or were taught in our childhood, learning to navigate our thoughts, looking at our shadow self, practicing forgiveness, exploring all our "human muck" is all necessary work to live more in alignment with Source. The benefits outweigh any potential discomfort. This is the way to higher consciousness and a better life.

Affirm

I am ready to dive into my spiritual work.
I can do hard things.
I am safe, even when I feel discomfort.
I can thrive while learning to love myself.
I am fully supported and loved.
I am learning that I am a divine being.

SOME THOUGHTS ABOUT THOUGHTS
MAY 13

"Thoughts are things" is a popular New Thought phrase that encourages us to remember that everything that exists started first as a thought. This phrase helps us remember to notice our thoughts, see them as something we can control, manage, and use as tools in our manifestation journey. Our thoughts are creative and powerful.

A similar New Thought saying that helps us understand this even more, says: "Thoughts *cause* things." Thoughts don't actually do the creating, but our thoughts are what the Universe responds to in the Creative Process. The Universe uses our thoughts to create our experience. This is God in action, in you. The Creative Process is working in you because of your thoughts.

Affirm

My thoughts are powerful, so I choose to think mindfully.

YOUR SPIRITUAL SELF
MAY 14

Often, we are reluctant to give our attention to the spiritual reality that is unfolding around us, through us, and in us. We say things like, "Well, when everything else fails, I guess I'll give God a try. When I've exhausted all other options, then I'll explore my spiritual side." Too often, we save the Divine as our Hail Mary act of desperation.

If we put our attention on our true spiritual divine nature first, by acknowledging God, Spirit, Universe, Source (or whatever we choose to call It), developing a spiritual practice, studying spiritual principles and applying them to our life, that's when peaceful, easy living has the potential to unfold. Spend some time getting to know your spiritual self. It is your God-Self. It is how we live our best life. Here are some tips for getting to know your spiritual self:

Act

Spend time alone
Experience and appreciate nature
Identify your feelings
Meditate
Journal
Serve others/volunteer
Practice self-care
Accept the present moment
Connect with a spiritual community

IT'S OKAY TO START SMALL
MAY 15

The Universe doesn't know the difference between manifesting something small and manifesting something huge. The principle is the same either way, whether you want to manifest ten dollars or ten million dollars. Starting small can boost our confidence and faith.

When I first discovered New Thought principles, I started by manifesting parking spots—something small, unimportant, and frankly, insignificant. Every time I went to a coffee shop, a grocery store, the shopping center, anywhere—I would use my spiritual practice. I would visualize. I would imagine what it would feel like to have a front row spot available to me as soon as I got there. I would say out loud, "Thank you, Universe!" when, inevitably, I started getting front row parking spots all the time.

Manifesting is like a muscle. At the gym, we start by lifting small weights first, until our muscles adapt and the weights become easy. Then we move to the bigger, heavier weights. We build our skills by manifesting small things at first. We do this because of our humanness. Think of it as allowing our human mind the time to more fully understand the enormous power of the One Mind. It is okay to start with parking spots, or ten dollars, or any other small thing you want to see and experience in your life.

Act

The Universe doesn't know the difference.
Once you get good at the small stuff, go bigger, dream bigger!

TIME TO S.T.O.P

MAY 16

When siblings are young, a common scenario happens—they fight and bicker. In the midst of the battle, they each insist the other one started the conflict. There are screams of, "He started it!" and "No, she did!" Often, a frustrated parent steps in and says something like, "I don't care who started it. I'm stopping it. Now!" The fighting stops because the parent says to stop.

S.T.O.P. can be an important tool for anyone handling conflict—from young children to leaders of nations. From a spiritual perspective, S.T.O.P. stands for "Surrender To One Power." Choosing to Surrender To One Power means you stop what you are doing. You stop talking, stop yelling, stop fighting, and stop reacting. Surrendering to One Power does not mean you give up your personal power. It means you stop and check in with the Divine. Surrendering is about knowing the Truth of your divine nature, allowing it to enter your awareness, and being in the flow of what is revealed to you.

It doesn't matter what you call this One Power, or what religion you affiliate It with. The One Power, One Presence, One Life is everything and everyone. It is everywhere. It is all life. It is the oneness of all humanity.

Affirm

Today, I choose to S.T.O.P. and surrender to the One Power of all that is.
I am one with God. I am one with all life.

ENDLESS SUPPLY FROM SOURCE
MAY 17

What is the source of your prosperity and abundance? Is it your job, your paycheck, the income you receive from business transactions or investments? Not really. The reality is, God is your source. In fact, *Source* is one of the words used for God. God is the source of everything, of all our good.

The Bible tells us not to worry about our food or clothing, because all our needs are met in God. If the birds don't worry about their abundance because their needs are met, then neither should we (Luke 12:22-24). If God provides for nature in this way, then surely God provides for us as well. When we fully understand who and what the source of our good really is, it becomes a manifestation tool. We can confidently trust in our abundance because God's very nature is an endless supply of abundance. Abundance is all around, moving to, through, and in you.

Affirm

All my needs are met in God, the One Infinite Supply of all my good.

WHAT ARE THOSE BELIEFS?
MAY 18

New Thought teaches us to pay attention to our beliefs and to make note of any false beliefs we may have. Then, it encourages us to change them. The problem with beliefs is, sometimes we aren't even aware we have them! For example, if a child is told that she is stupid, that she will never become anything, she will likely grow up clinging to that belief into adulthood. She might not even realize where it came from. Alternatively, if a child is told that he can do anything, that he is very smart and brilliant, he will likely grow up and turn into an adult who holds this wonderful belief.

Figuring out what our beliefs are, where they originated, and why is tricky. We really have to deeply examine our childhood beliefs. When we do, we often discover those beliefs simply don't serve us as adults. What we were taught to believe as children directly influences the kind of life we lead as adults. The good news is that beliefs can always be changed to be more in alignment with your spiritual Truth. This is the spiritual work of life.

Ask

What was I told as a child?
What beliefs were modeled for me?
What was my experience with not only parents,
but grandparents, siblings, teachers, friends, and clergy?

STATE YOUR FAITH
MAY 19

A statement of faith in a Universal God using positive affirmations:

Affirm

I am free to follow spiritual principles that resonate with me.
I am free to do what works for me in this moment.
I release the past and step into a new, greater understanding of the Divine.
I write my own story, think my own thoughts, form my own beliefs,
and develop my own attitudes.
I am always seeking to express my true divine nature, which is God's nature.
Spirit is here with me in this moment and in every moment.
I am surrounded, supported, and loved.
I know the Truth, and the Truth sets me free!

LOVE MEDITATION
MAY 20

Take a moment to pause and meditate on love.

Act

Take a deep breath in. Let it out slowly through your mouth. Shift your attention to your heart space—the space at the center of your being where you know that all is well. Imagine your heart opening and receiving the Love of the Universe as glowing white light. Your heart is open from the front, and the love pours in. It is open from behind, the love is flooding in. It is open on the top, the bottom, and on all sides; love fills your entire being. Love flows in and through you in a gentle rushing motion of light.

You receive this love, and you give this love easily. It can never be all used up; there is an endless, flowing supply of love. Imagine this and feel this. You are the Divine Love and Light of God.

WHAT YOU CAN'T SEE
MAY 21

The Divine Science Statement of Being[*] has a line that reads: "God is all, the invisible and the visible." That means God is everything we can see and everything we can't see. Do you realize how much we *can't* see? It boggles the mind to comprehend or even imagine because we can't see it! It's like walking up to someone and demanding, "Tell me everything you don't know!" What a silly thing to ask! Trying to think of everything you can't see is just as crazy. But this is exactly the point. The purpose of the challenge is to better understand the universality and totality of the Divine. It is so much bigger and better than we could possibly fathom. God. Is. All.

Act

Take this thought into contemplation, meditation, and reflection.

---

[*] James, F. B., & Cramer, M. E. (1957). *Divine Science; Its Principles and Practice. compiled from Truth and Health, by Fannie B. James and Divine Science and Healing, by Malinda E. Cramer*. Textbook of Divine Science.

HOW INSPIRING!
MAY 22

When you are inspired, you are in-Spirit. When you get those moments of inspiration, good ideas, and ingenious thoughts, it's because you are in-Spirit, living in alignment and fully aware of the divine nature within you, expressing as you. Another way to look at it is to remember the origin of the word *spirit*, which comes from the Latin *spiritus*, which means "a breathing." This is where the English word *respiration* comes from. When inspiration strikes, you are being breathed by Spirit. Spirit is in action, moving in you, divinely influencing your thoughts, words, and actions.

You can live in a state of mind, a state of consciousness, where you are constantly open to divine inspiration. Be aware of your oneness and unity with Source; remind yourself of this Truth. Invite inspiration and guidance into your daily practice.

Affirm

At any moment, I can shift my attention to God; I am ready to be inspired!

BEYOND LUCK
MAY 23

Isn't it funny how the person you know who insists they are unlucky always seems to encounter unlucky experiences? Things go wrong for them, problems spring up, and then they say something like, "See? I told you I was unlucky! This is what always happens to me!" They demonstrate confirmation bias, which means they interpret new evidence as confirmation of their existing beliefs.

From an objective standpoint, it is easy to see this is also a bad habit—a habit of claiming bad luck and looking for an unlucky experience. It is a habit of thought, but a habit of thought can be changed. When you change the habit of a bad thought, you alter your life. All we have to do is notice the pattern and be willing to change.

Affirm

It is never too late to think a new thought and change a bad habit.

THIS IS TRUE OF YOU
MAY 24

The following is a Spiritual Mind Treatment to recognize our divine nature.

Pray

What I know to be true is that God is all there is. There is only One Power, One Presence, One Life. It's God's Life. I express as the One Life of God. This is true for everyone.

That means the qualities, traits, and attributes of God: Love, Peace, Joy, Balance, Abundance, Health, Wholeness, Creativity—those are my qualities and traits. They are my divine nature, and they are true for my life. That is what I am focused on, that is where I put my attention. That is how I wish to live my life and what I expect and anticipate my experience to be (Love, Peace, Joy, Balance, Abundance, Health, Wholeness, Creativity, etc.) What is true of God is true of me.

I give great thanks for this. I am so grateful that I understand this is the way Life works. There is nothing more to do but release this prayer and let it unfold joyously.

And So It Is. Amen.

VISUALIZE YOUR RESULTS
MAY 25

Have you ever had a serious medical test done, and you had to wait several days for the results? It can be a harrowing, anxiety-filled experience. You want to hope for the best, but your mind can run away with you, as you imagine the worst. This is where a spiritual principle like visualization can help you actively imagine the outcome you want to see.

Will the results come by phone? Imagine the call, being told all is clear, everything looks good. How will you feel when you hear that? Can you replicate the scenario in your mind until you feel the relief and excitement in your body? Will the results come by email or in a website portal update? Write out the script you want to see. See the scans as clear and the test results as favorable. Immerse yourself in a great outcome. Daydream about it, journal about it, sit with it in meditation, and fall asleep to thoughts of your perfect health and wholeness. This is what it means to work the principles.

Affirm

Today, I visualize the outcome I wish to see.
I am never at the mercy of my circumstances.

WOW!
MAY 26

There is a popular meme that circulates on social media that says: "We all live on one big rock, floating through space, and you still don't believe in miracles?" The point of the message is, of course, that our very existence is miraculous. Author Anne Lamott wrote a book called *"Help, Thanks, Wow: The Three Essential Prayers."* * The Wow category is about living in and praying from a state of awe at the world around us. It is a vital part of our spiritual awareness. We can (and should) be in awe daily, seeing all the parts of our existence for what they are—miracles!

Our next breath is a miracle. The sunrise is a miracle. Human love is a miracle. The electrical impulse that beats your heart is a miracle. The birth of a baby is a miracle. A seed that sprouts and eventually grows into a tree is a miracle. Animal instinct is a miracle. Consciousness is a miracle. Because of all this and so much more, miracles (and all things) are possible. We live in a universe of limitless miracles. Believe in them; they are all around us!

Affirm

I believe in miracles!

---

* Lamott, A. (2019). *Help, Thanks, Wow: The Three Essential Prayers*. Penguin Publishing

ON A REGULAR BASIS
MAY 27

Thessalonians 5:17 tells us to pray unceasingly. Does that mean we are to spend every day on our knees, with our eyes closed, deep in prayer? Of course not, because that isn't realistic. Prayer is acknowledging not just our unity with God, but the Truth of our higher self, and the Truth that we are surrounded and supported by a loving Spirit. We are never alone in this life. Can you be aware of this throughout the day? Doing so is like strengthening and building up a muscle when we go to the gym. Stretching and working out our muscles is practice for when we need them. Praying and shifting our awareness to God is "spiritual practice." When we practice connecting with our spiritual aspects regularly, unceasingly, it becomes easier to receive guidance, answers, revelations, and inspiration.

Affirm

I am never alone. I am surrounded and supported by Love.

NOT MY FORTE
MAY 28

Have you ever had to do something far out of your comfort zone—something that is not in your particular skill set? I once had to put together a piece of furniture, and the directions had no words, only pictures. I put it together in a way that the top was backward, and the item was not usable. My husband came along and, after glancing at the instructions for just a moment, he immediately took it apart and put it together perfectly. He is mechanically inclined, great at manual dexterity, and has exceptional spatial awareness. I am not like him. I need words and clearly written instructions!

What I *can* do, however, is write inspirational books, give motivational presentations, and help people understand complex spiritual concepts through language. That is *my* skill set. We are all different. All our brains work differently. There is a good reason for that. We are all expressions of Spirit. That is perhaps the point of life—we are here to help each other. We need each other. That is the Truth of our harmony and oneness.

Affirm

*Today, I acknowledge all the beautiful ways
Spirit expresses Itself in me, through me, and as me.*

SMOOTH SAILING
MAY 29

Sailboats experience drag and resistance as they move through the water. Sailors must feel the unseen force of the water. An experienced sailor can feel it, align with it, and intuitively know what to do to navigate the waves and make their way. It could be a tough, stormy wind or a gentle breeze. It could be rough or smooth sailing.

Such is the nature of life. Whatever resistance we encounter, whatever conditions and circumstances we may experience, we can tune into it all and adjust our sails accordingly. We can always, *always* adjust our thought and align our consciousness with the One Consciousness of God.

Affirm

*I expect and anticipate smooth sailing
as I remain steadfast in my unity and oneness with God*

RIGHT NOW, EXPRESS IT
MAY 30

New babies and infants are so joyous and wonderful; they are full of life and love. Babies don't spend any time worrying about the future or getting upset about the past. It is always *right now* for a baby. They are experts at living in the present moment. They ask for what they want when they want it, and they are very good at expressing their feelings. If a baby is angry, everyone is going to know it is angry! But then, moments later, if a baby is happy, you will know that, too. They don't hold on to their emotions; they express the feeling and move on almost instantly.

Can we adults say the same? Somewhere along the line, many of us turned into adults who don't express our feelings. Here are some tips for expressing our feelings, releasing trapped emotions, and living in the now.

Act

Have the tantrum.
Write an angry letter and destroy it.
Punch the pillow.
Exercise through your emotions.
Talk to a trusted friend.

THE QUIET WHEELS
MAY 31

Nobody walks around thinking, "Gee, I'm so grateful that I don't have a toothache today!" or, "Gee, I'm so thankful that my body is digesting my food properly!" We don't think about the high-functioning health, intelligence, and wisdom of the body that is happening inside us. Instead of focusing on our health and wholeness, we're focused on the problem we're experiencing, the symptom, the illness, the disease. It is the squeaky wheel of our pain that gets our attention, yet Spiritual Law tells us that what we focus on and think about expands. Why would we ever want to focus on pain and illness? We certainly don't want more of that. We draw to us more health and wholeness when we're focused on our health and wholeness. Surely we want to focus on these ideas!

Act

When you go to sleep at night, take the opportunity to mentally go through your body and give thanks for all the things that are working properly. From your head to your toes, consider all your body systems: your organs, bones, blood, muscles, and joints, down to every tiny cell in your body that is expressing perfect Divine Wholeness. Give thanks for it all.

JUNE

PRIDE IN ALL
JUNE 1

For centuries, religions have painted a picture of the Divine as a masculine father figure, and most refer to God as "Father." Some progressive, more liberal faith traditions use words like "Father-Mother-God," or even neutral pronouns like "It" when referring to the One Power of the Divine. What we know to be true is that God is ALL—every gender, no gender, and everything in between. God is bigger and more encompassing than any human expression of biological sex, gender identity, and expression.

Spirit can only create things out of Itself. That is all it has to work with. We are all made of God stuff. The Divine is expressing as each one of us individually. There are no mistakes. There are no wrong expressions. It is not possible for there to be a wrong expression. Every one of us is like God, looking at Itself in the mirror. I am you. You are me. We are all God.

Lesbian = God. Homosexual = God. Bisexual = God. Transgender = God. Queer = God. Cisgender = God. Intersex = God. Nonbinary = God. Genderfluid = God. Asexual = God. Binary = God. Androgynous = God. Heterosexual = God. Any human expression you can possibly think of and label = God.

Happy Pride Month.

Affirm

All life is beautiful.

WHEN PRAYING FOR RAIN
JUNE 2

A story is told of a village that was experiencing a terrible drought. For months, temperatures soared, the sun scorched the crops, and the risk of fire increased. The villagers went to the spiritual leaders, seeking their help. Their response was simple: "We must pray for rain!" The leaders arranged a gathering in the middle of town so everyone could come together and pray for rain. The whole community showed up… but only one little girl thought to bring an umbrella.

That is the faith of a child!

You have heard the term "childlike faith." It is a real thing and a powerful concept. Children can suspend their belief in reality and play make-believe wholly. They are more receptive to Divine Truth than most adults. They believe in invisible things without hesitation. This is evident when you have a child who is convinced they have an invisible friend as a playmate when no one is there.

We can't necessarily see God's Truth of goodness, wholeness, abundance, peace, and love. But when we believe in these things fully, wholly, with our entire being, Spiritual Law has no choice but to demonstrate them into our experience. Our good is already here, already available to us.

Act

When praying for rain, remember to grab your umbrella and get ready for it!
The faith of a child demonstrates it.

DRAW THE CIRCLE WIDE
JUNE 3

There is an old saying that asserts: "Different strokes for different folks." It simply means that different ways of doing something can be appropriate for different people—different things appeal to different people. As someone who has studied Interfaith, Religious Science, and New Thought ministry, I see how this saying correlates to our spiritual journey.

We can honor all the different paths to the Divine. We can seek out and find the Divine in a way that resonates for us individually, while allowing and accepting other people's paths, methods, rituals, and understanding. Tolerance, allowance, and grace toward the spirituality of others are really about acceptance, growth, and our choice to draw the circle of God wider and bigger.

Affirm

Today, I celebrate the myriad of ways the one Universal God appeals to each of us.

LET IT COME TO YOU
JUNE 4

Have you ever tried to catch a butterfly or find a ladybug? You run and jump around as the butterfly happily flits and flies away from you. You scour the ground searching in vain for a tiny ladybug until you finally give up. When we give up these tiring endeavors, something interesting happens. In our stillness, our calmness, these amazing creatures we seek are drawn to us.

If you sit or lie still, you might discover that a butterfly has landed on your shoulder, your leg, or even your nose! You may look down at your arm to see a tiny ladybug happily crawling on you. This is a great reminder that manifestation works in the same way. Yes, we need to stay focused on our goals, looking for our good, but we must do this with balance. There is a time to relax and be still in a state of expectancy and certainty. What you wish to have, do, or be is already yours. It is on its way to you now.

Act

Be still.

WORRY ABOUT YOURSELF
JUNE 5

Do you believe you can influence the behavior of the collective and lift the consciousness of the world? I think we can. We do this by spending time in higher consciousness. Consider this example:

Many years ago, I taught elementary school. When you have a bunch of kindergartners, first graders, or second graders (that age group), and they are tattling on each other, what does a teacher inevitably say? "Worry about yourself. Don't worry about that other kid; just focus on your own behavior." One child's mindfulness causes a ripple effect through the group. The idea is, if you get all the kids to turn within and pay attention to what they are doing for themselves, the behavior of the whole group begins to improve and change for the better.

Spending time in higher consciousness is sometimes all we can do to help the world. You might not be a world leader who can negotiate peace talks and navigate change. You might not be a famous activist who can influence large numbers of people. That's okay. Focus on yourself. Regular folks like you and I can focus on our own higher consciousness through our spiritual practice, reading inspirational spiritual texts like this one, journaling, praying, meditating, etc.

Affirm

Every moment I spend in higher consciousness uplifts the consciousness of the world.

WHAT IS MEDITATION?
JUNE 6

Meditation is a word that gets thrown around a lot in spiritual circles as a useful spiritual practice, but what does it really mean to meditate? It can mean different things to different people, and you can do it in a variety of ways. Focused in thought? You're meditating. Sitting in silence? You're meditating. Attempting to relax as you breathe deeply? Yes, that is meditation, too. Mentally trying to connect to a higher power as you lie motionless? That is meditation as well. Chanting as you attempt to clear your mind? Yes, that's meditation. Listening to a guided story that encourages you to use your imagination? That is a type of meditation. Feeling calm and peaceful when resting after your yoga practice? Yes, that is a meditative state. Using an app, visiting a meditation website, or listening to music? Yes, yes, yes. Meditation is a broad spectrum of activities that involve your attention, your awareness, and your mind/body connection.

Act

Choosing to practice meditation is more important than the method you choose.

WHAT'S THE LESSON HERE?
JUNE 7

Think about a problem or situation that is frustrating you. Stop and ask yourself: "If Spirit sent this problem, why? What am I supposed to learn from it? What is this trying to teach me? What is the message in this experience?" Have a conversation with your inner self and then listen for a response.

Spirit does not send problems, but it is amazing how, when we open ourselves to the idea of a relationship with the Divine, we can be guided and led through life's difficulties. We can navigate our challenges and receive help. We don't have to be frustrated and angry and spin our wheels over our problems. Divine Wisdom is always available; it simply takes our awareness. Step back and take a breath.

Ask

What do I need to know?
How am I supposed to respond?
What am I supposed to learn?
What is my gut saying?
What is my intuition telling me?

Affirm

I have a relationship with Spirit, and I am always willing to learn.

USE YOUR TOOLBOX
JUNE 8

In our moments of pain, anxiety, and fear, we can use our spiritual skills to heal and feel whole again. It is important not to let negative human conditions distract you, get you down, or destroy you. There have been many instances in my life where I have had to physically remove myself from a situation. I quite literally excused myself and demanded a secluded moment alone.

What do I do in these moments? I consciously remind myself of my Truth. Sometimes that looks like me rocking myself to sleep, or crying through my deep breaths, or chanting in a whisper repeatedly that "God is here, God is here, God is here." Sometimes it looks like me stopping to journal and write down the outcome I wish to see. It can be my call or text to a prayer partner for support. Sometimes it is my own prayer echoing in the chamber of my mind. It can be a soothing guided meditation through noise-canceling headphones.

The point is, you have a toolbox, too. You are loved, supported, and full of wisdom. Use the spiritual practices available to you.

Ask

What is in my spiritual toolbox?

TURN TO YOUR CONSCIOUSNESS
JUNE 9

One of the tenets of New Thought says, "Your life experiences are a reflection of your consciousness." Our consciousness is our mental awareness, the sum of our thoughts and beliefs about anything and everything. Our spiritual beliefs are, of course, a part of it, but it's much more than that. Our consciousness creates our experience. An example might be, if you firmly believe that a trip to the doctor is awful, that it involves a long wait, intrusive tests, ineffective employees, and a diagnosis of disease, then the Universe will reflect that to you. If you are convinced of this and believe strongly in that outcome of difficulties, this scenario is likely what you will experience the next time you go to the doctor.

Everyone wants a good, easy life free from problems. So, how do we use our consciousness to create this for ourselves? When you are experiencing something you don't like (illness, lack, frustration, problems with your job, any kind of trouble) it is just the Universe telling you to pay attention to your consciousness. Notice what you are thinking and believing about your life. What inner dialogue are you having? This philosophy is never taught from a place of judgment or blame. It never suggests that you created your problems, and you are left on your own. This mindful self-reflection is a tool to use. When you are uncomfortable and frustrated with your life experience, it is an indicator to turn to your consciousness, thoughts, and beliefs. Consider what is at the root of it all.

Affirm

It is safe to mindfully explore my consciousness.

CELEBRATE THEIR SUCCESS
JUNE 10

Do you ever look at another person's success and feel a spark of jealousy? We all have, but here is a little spiritual manifestation trick. You can use other people's success to your own advantage. There is an unlimited supply of abundance available to everyone, and that includes you. When you see someone else who is successful, you can use their success as a mental equivalent. You can look at their success, bless them, be happy for them, and think to yourself, "Wow, if they can achieve that, if they can receive that abundance, then so can I."

Their success is just another mental equivalent that is available for you to see, think about, and believe is possible. Instead of a jealous thought, your affirmation can be, *"I can have that too!"* Celebrate other people's success and abundance, trusting there is enough for all.

Affirm

Today, I celebrate all success, for it is part of living an abundant life.

BE THE THING
JUNE 11

A spiritual lesson suggests that whatever it is you feel you are missing or lacking in your life, if you *be* that thing in the world, it helps you attract it into your life. For instance, if you want to experience more love, ask yourself where or to whom you can be loving. If you feel you are lacking abundance, consider where you can be generous and give of your time, talents, and treasure. If you desire to experience health in your body, think about what healthy parts of your body you can cultivate, celebrate, and honor.

The Law of Attraction suggests that like attracts like. People tend to attract experiences, situations, and people that are similar to their own thoughts, emotions, and vibrational energy. Be the thing you desire, even if only in your mind. Act as if it is so, and so it shall be.

Affirm

I <u>am</u> whatever I desire.

FEAR IS A THOUGHT
JUNE 12

If you feel fear about something, it helps to remember that fear is just a thought. Yes, the fear feels very real, to the point we might believe it, and let it consume us. But the truth is, fear is only a thought in your mind that you created. You can, in this moment and in any moment, decide to no longer feel fear about whatever the thing is you are fearing. You can decide that. You have the free will to make that decision, and you can put your complete and total faith in a new thought.

Affirm

My fear is a thought, and a thought can be changed.
I am safe, and all is well.

THIS TOO SHALL PASS
JUNE 13

In case you forgot, you are eternal. Life is eternal. If you are reading this, then that means you are alive. If you are alive, then you are divine and part of nature. This experience as a human being is temporary. Whatever it is that is stressing you out, distracting you, and feels like a very big deal… it probably isn't. Life is so much bigger than our human problems that we have to manage. For just a moment, set your problems down and rest in the Truth that you are an eternal soul. Walk a little taller and smile a little wider, knowing this.

Affirm

In this moment, I trust in the Truth of capital-L-Life.
I am eternal.

DON'T FORGET TO ASK
JUNE 14

We know that when we are seeking guidance, direction, clarity, or wisdom from the Divine, we have to ask. The asking is part of an important surrendering that facilitates our receiving. Asking is acknowledging our relationship and our unity with the Divine. Asking puts us in a place of our willingness to receive. Don't forget to ask.

Whether it is done through meditation or prayer or journaling or quiet contemplating or whatever spiritual practice you engage in, ask the Spirit within you for guidance, wisdom, and clarity. Our human life is always an opportunity for relationship with the Divine. Let today serve as a chance to cultivate this relationship and ask for a revelation of Spirit. We receive by first being brave enough, bold enough, and most of all, *willing* to ask.

Affirm

Today, I remember to ask for that which I wish to receive.

YOUR WAY IS MADE CLEAR
JUNE 15

Next time you are traveling, whether by car, airplane, cruise, or train, say this affirmation and set the following intention: *My way is made clear.* Set aside some time to take that phrase into your meditation or prayer before your trip. Perhaps think about the Hindu deity Ganesha, who is known as the remover of obstacles. The Power and Presence of the Divine, whether Ganesha, or God, Spirit, Universe, Source, whatever we want to call it, is present with you always, removing anything out of your way. When you move from this mindset, nothing could possibly obstruct your travel. Consciously intend to have a wonderful experience, arriving at your destination safely.

Affirm

My way is made clear. I am divinely guided and protected.

YOU DESERVE THE BEST
JUNE 16

What do you really think and believe about what you deserve in life? Pause over each of these words and see what comes up for you with regard to whether they are expressing in your life: Abundance. Love. Health. Prosperity. Harmony. Creativity. Opportunity. Joy. Intelligence. Wholeness.

Too often, we live in our humanness, completely unaware of what we are thinking, believing, and creating. An unclear, muddled consciousness reflects unclear, muddled demonstrations. Thoughts and beliefs can be changed. Our willingness is the first step toward living in alignment with our true nature.

Affirm

*My mind is calm, focused, and aligned
with my best self, my higher consciousness.
I deserve to live my best life.*

JOURNALING AS SPIRITUAL PRACTICE
JUNE 17

Journaling is a very effective spiritual practice. I used to think it was a waste of time, but what changed my mind was when I made a commitment to the practice. I committed to writing three pages a day, for one month, to start. Sometimes, I had to force myself. I began by writing letters to God in my journal. Was I complaining sometimes? Yes. Was I whining about changes that I wanted to see happen in my life? Yes. Did I write a lot of nonsense? Absolutely. Eventually, once I was used to the habit, I learned how to use my journal as a way to declare and affirm the life I desired. I wrote as if the outcomes I wished to see had already happened.

Journaling is like a muscle and a skill that builds over time with practice. When you add journaling to your spiritual practice repertoire, it helps you build your relationship with the Divine. God, Spirit, the Universe, Source, your angels, guides, and ancestors are all your partners. Write to them. Dialogue with them. Ask them for help. You will receive the answers, guidance, direction, and clarity you are seeking.

Ask

What would I say to God in a letter?
What questions would I ask?

ONE LIGHT
JUNE 18

Relax your body. Relax the muscles around your eyes. Relax your jaw. Roll your shoulders back. Imagine all the muscles in your body softening the way butter does when it comes to room temperature. Take in a nice, deep breath. Blow it out slowly through your mouth. Imagine your body being filled with light. It starts from the beating of your heart and spreads out to your entire body. Now, imagine all the other people on earth as beings of light, filled with the Love and Light of the Divine.

Imagine the collective of humanity filled with the Light of the Divine, and within each individual being is the peace, the harmony, and the love of God. Imagine this light in all of us getting stronger and brighter, connecting each of us together, as if we are recognizing ourselves in one another. This is our Truth, our harmony, and our oneness. Our awareness of this feeling is what changes the world. We lift our own individual consciousness. Together, we lift the consciousness of the world, realizing at last that there is only One Consciousness. Let us stand in this Truth and give great thanks.

Affirm

I am the Light. You are the Light.
We are the One Light of God.

WHY ARE YOU HERE?
JUNE 19

Some deep, existential questions to consider:

Ask

If my soul chose to be here at this time in history, why?
Why am I here?
Am I here for a divine purpose?
(Spoiler alert: YOU ARE.)

Act

Think about this:
Right now, whatever year it is, whatever time in history it is,
you are here for a reason.

HOW WILL IT FEEL?
JUNE 20

Do you imagine the worst possible outcome when you are worried? Do you obsess about the worst-case scenario? Your imagination is very powerful. Use it for good. Imagine the best outcome that you want to see, that you want to experience. If you don't know what that looks like, that's okay. Imagine how you want to feel in whatever outcome you wish to see. How are you going to *feel*? Imagine it in your mind and see if you can get yourself to feel it in your body.

How are you going to feel when the best possible outcome happens? That is how we manifest the reality we want to see. Your thoughts are powerful, but your feelings are magnetic. Draw your good to you.

Affirm

Today, I am focused on feeling the good I wish to experience.

DREAMS THAT YOU DARE TO DREAM
JUNE 21

A lovely song from the movie *The Wizard of Oz* suggests that our dreams come true somewhere outside of us, or somewhere "over the rainbow." Of course, this isn't really true. The dreams that we dare to dream come true when we start to believe they can come true. Our belief is the key to manifesting anything we wish to experience.

Our belief is powerful, and it can only come from deep within us. Our dreams do not materialize because an outside force magically intervenes on our behalf. We are completely unified with the One Power of God, and we cannot be separated from it. We have the power to draw our good to us, revealing the experience we desire. Believe in the possibility of your dreams coming true.

Affirm

All things are possible because the unlimited potential of the Divine is within me.

YOUR SIMPLE CHOICE
JUNE 22

Only you are in charge of your thoughts and beliefs. No news program can tell you what to think. No church can tell you what to believe. No doctor can tell you how to think about your body's health. No employer can tell you what to believe. No parent can take charge of your thoughts and beliefs. You have free will because you exist, and that free will contains all the power you need.

You can choose to think and believe anything you want. Why make it hard or complicated? Think and believe good things about your life. Affirm good things. Speak good things. Believe good things. Act as if good things are already occurring. It really is that simple.

Affirm

Today, I choose to keep it simple: My life is good!

SHOW UP AS PEACE
JUNE 23

When you look at the world around you and feel uncertain or scared due to events outside your control, there is something you can do to reassure yourself. You can consciously decide to show up in the world as peace. We are expressions of the Divine. That means, we have the opportunity to show up as the qualities of the Divine. Peace is a quality of the Divine. Chaos is not divine, and it never can be.

Things may look chaotic in the world, but you have a choice in how you think, speak, and act. Become hyperaware of this choice today. Choose peace. Choose peace in your thoughts, in your mind, in your activities, and in all your interactions. Carry with you in your awareness a consciousness of peace.

Affirm

*I am the Peace of God, and I consciously
choose to express as peace in the world.*

WELCOME HOME
JUNE 24

Remember the last time you came home from a vacation or traveling, and you felt like you could finally exhale and relax? You were back to being in your own house and sleeping in your own bed. It felt so good to be home because it was comfortable and familiar. That is the way it will feel when we make our physical transition. It is possible that this is what our "death" is like. (Note: There is no death; life is eternal. It is a transition back to our true self, our spiritual self.) It will feel so comfortable and so serene, like we can truly relax back into our soul form.

Whenever we travel and return home, it gives us a little glimpse of that experience because it feels so good to be back in our comfort zone. Remember, your true comfort zone, your true self, is your spiritual soul, and it is eternal. This human life is wonderful and temporary.

Affirm

Someday, I will be welcomed back home to my true self.

EVERYTHING IS WITHIN
JUNE 25

Everything you could possibly need and want is within you. You are that powerful, that well-supplied, and that loved. Do you worry about your life? Worrying is a misuse of Spiritual Law, with often negative demonstration results. Why not use your attention, study, and thoughts to remember the Truth? All your needs are met. Trust that everything you need is available to you. What you seek is seeking you.

Ask

Can I live today as if everything I desire is already available to me? What changes would this make in my attitude?

LOVE IS CLOSE
JUNE 26

Love is always closer than you think. If you look around your life, at your experiences and your circumstances, there is love buried in there somewhere. If you are convinced it's not there, consider this. Most, if not all, religious teachings tell us that the One Power and Presence of God is everywhere. If God is everywhere, and God is Love, then by extension, love must be everywhere. But do you see it? Answered honestly, sometimes we don't. We see hate, war, injustice, pain, lack, confusion, and suffering—a collective humanity in need of God's Love.

What if we looked at love from a scientific perspective? Just like God, energy is everywhere. Consider the energy of light, sound, motion, heat, and electricity, etc. Energy always exists all around us, but if we are not paying attention to it, connected to it, aware of it, actively using it, we miss out on the experience of it. If you are looking for love, and you're not seeing it, it may be your opportunity to *be* the love. Find ways to immerse yourself in love for yourself.

Affirm

Love is always closer than I think because love is who and what I am.

REWRITE YOUR LIFE
JUNE 27

Years ago, I used to teach elementary school, and in my classroom, I had a giant whiteboard that you would use dry-erase markers with. Inevitably, some student would get a hold of a permanent Sharpie™ marker and write or draw something on the board (usually something disgusting that I did not want permanently on my whiteboard), so I would be tasked with the job of removing it. How did I do it?

I took the dry-erase marker and wrote over whatever was drawn or written on the whiteboard, covering it completely, and then I erased it with an eraser. Somehow, that permanent ink of the Sharpie™ marker attaches to the dry-erase marker ink, and the eraser can erase it all.

This is a spiritual lesson. The permanent marker is like a stain, a mistake, a "sin," a misuse of Spiritual Law. Using the correct tools, using Spiritual Law correctly, being in alignment with Source, applying spiritual principles, and knowing the Truth of our divine nature help us eliminate, erase, and get rid of any mistake.

Affirm

I have the tools within me to rewrite my life.

YOUR PERFECT LIFE
JUNE 28

God, Spirit, the Universe, Source, no matter what we call it, does not promise you a perfect life. What would that even look like? A perfect life would inevitably be decided by "human standards." If I said, "Describe your perfect life," everyone would have a different answer. Perfect according to whom? We are not promised that kind of perfection. What we are promised is that we are perfect. There is a difference. Your eternal soul, your eternal being-ness, the Truth of your divine nature, is perfect.

That is a big realization. Take it in for today. You are not broken. You are not flawed. You are not faulty, inadequate, or inferior. You are perfect at the core of your being.

Affirm

(Say it out loud and proud.)
I am perfect.

THAT'S IT
JUNE 29

God is not something to believe in.
God is something you are.

That's it. This the message for the day.

Act

Take this thought into contemplation, meditation, and reflection.

ABUNDANCE IN NATURE
JUNE 30

The key to attracting more abundance is to think abundantly. Abundance is a quality of God, and therefore, it is everywhere. Consider nature. There is an abundance of outer space; just look at the billions of stars in the sky. There is an unlimited number of grains of sand on a beach. A constantly replenished supply of oxygen is available on the planet. There is abundance in everything if we are willing to acknowledge it. God's very nature is abundance in general, unlimited resources, wealth, and opportunities.

Humans are part of nature. There is an abundance of good within you. Why would you be on this planet if you were not intended to experience and express abundantly as all the good that exists? Our willingness to participate in the law of abundance is the only thing that limits our ability to receive. How is your mindset?

Affirm

Today, I choose to think big, think plenty, and think abundance.

JULY

PRINCIPLE OF HEALING
JULY 1

Imagine you are chopping some vegetables for dinner, and you're in a rush. The knife slips and nicks the edge of your finger. The cut isn't that deep, but it is definitely bleeding. You stop what you're doing, wash your hands, and get a Band-Aid.

Question: Would your finger heal? Of course it would. We don't think twice about healing a cut finger. Our bodies are designed to heal. It's how they work.

What if instead of a cut finger or broken bone, you were told you had arthritis? Or a lung infection? Heart disease? Cancer? A physical body is spiritually made, always striving to express as balance and perfect wholeness. The body can return to wholeness after cancer as easily as it can after a paper cut. The difference is not in the intensity of injury or disease, but in our degree of belief. This goes for everything. Five dollars' worth of abundance can be manifested as easily as five million dollars because the principle is the same. The only difference is the degree to which it is applied.

Perhaps the real lesson for humans is to stop thinking small. Stop believing in limitation. There is no limit to what you can heal from, achieve, accomplish, and receive.

Affirm

I release the idea of limitation. Healing is always possible.

SEEING WITH MAGIC EYES
JULY 2

In case you did not realize this, you are not a body. You *have* a body. You are a soul that is eternal. You are living today as a human being, in a body, temporarily, yet you are also a soul. You exist as both a body and a soul at the same time. It can be difficult to hold both ideas in your mind simultaneously.

Back in the 1990s, art pictures called autostereograms, known by the brand "Magic Eye," were all the rage. They contained duplicated images that you had to "look behind" to see a hidden 3D image. People would spend hours standing in Magic Eye art stores, staring at all the framed posters on the wall—hoping for a glimpse of the hidden picture inside the picture. It was a fun and sometimes frustrating activity. If you saw the concealed picture, it was often just for a few seconds before the duplicated images of the picture would come back into focus. That was the nature of the visual trick. Your eyes focus on slightly different points, and your brain takes in that information and perceives the hidden picture for just a second. The hidden picture isn't there, and then suddenly it is. Then just as suddenly, it isn't there again.

The Magic Eye puzzles are a great metaphor for how we understand the body/soul connection. Both are real. Both are you. Both are there at the same time. You are a body, and you are a soul.

Ask

Which one do I see at this moment?

NO COMPLAINTS HERE!
JULY 3

When we begin to grasp how powerful we are and understand our unlimited divine nature, we realize we truly have nothing to complain about! Why? Two reasons.

One, we hold all the power to change our lives. There is no reason to complain when we are the ones in charge of our thoughts. This would be like grumbling about the overly complicated, high-traffic route we took to work, knowing full well we were the one driving the car, making all the decisions. We are in charge!

The second reason there is nothing to complain about is that, much like worrying, complaining is a misuse of Spiritual Law! It draws to us more of what we don't like, don't need, and don't want. Remember, complaining is like telling Spirit, "I'll take more of this, please! I'd like some more of these problems to complain about." Our words are too powerful to be wasted on frivolous, foolish complaints.

Affirm

Today, I make the decision to go complaint-free and follow through with the effort to maintain the habit.

A PRAYER FOR FREEDOM
JULY 4

Pray

Knowing and trusting that there is only One Great Spirit of God, we declare our individual oneness and unity with It. Let our eyes be opened to the possibility of the grace within us dissolving our human, ego-based, manufactured problems. May we be reminded that every soul is born of God's goodness. What we want for ourselves, let us want and declare as true for everyone. We ask for help seeing the good of all and fully expect to experience its unfoldment. Let us see the Divine in every soul and consciously operate from a place of love. May this Truth set all people free. Solutions, abundance, and intelligence are present in this moment. We give great thanks for the continuous opportunity to show up as God's unconditional Love in this world.
And So It Is. Amen.

A GOOD IDEA
JULY 5

Repeat these words silently to yourself or speak them out loud:

I am an idea in the Mind of God.

How does that make you feel? This affirmation declares something good and true about yourself that you may have never considered. It is a unique perspective to perceive yourself in this way. Your soul, your body, your purpose, your personality—everything that makes up YOU—is an idea in the One Mind of God.

It makes sense that the Divine only has good ideas. How does it feel to know you are one of them? How could you be anything less than a brilliant idea in God's Mind? Hold your head a little higher and walk a little taller now that you understand this.

Affirm

I am an idea in the Mind of God.

A BEAUTIFUL CHANGE
JULY 6

When asked if childbirth is painful, it is likely that upward of 100% of mothers would say that yes, indeed, childbirth is painful. Labor is a series of continuous, progressive contractions that help the baby exit the birth canal and be born, and those contractions hurt. It is not known what triggers labor. For whatever reason, the old way of existing in the womb simply no longer works for the fetus. Things have to change. A woman in labor might say it feels like a violent upheaval and complete rebellion taking place in her own body.

Sometimes life is like this. The old ways of existing—the way we do things—cause problems, and they just don't work for us anymore. Change has to happen. Often, there is violence and upheaval. Change hurts. It is important to remember that the problems of this world cannot be solved in the same consciousness in which they were created. This is how we counteract the pain of transformation. The revolution still happens, but it is a revolution in thinking. We think differently, from a higher consciousness. We are less selfish, more unified, less violent, and more peaceful.

In the same way that painful childbirth leads to the beautiful new life of a baby, the painful changes that the world is collectively experiencing are leading to something good, something better.

Affirm

An awakening is happening.
I trust that a higher collective consciousness is unfolding.

PLANT YOUR SEEDS
JULY 7

I once bought a packet of sunflower seeds to plant in front of my house. I brought them home and set them on the kitchen counter, but I kept getting distracted and ended up ignoring them. When I noticed the packet still sitting there several weeks later, I said to my husband, "I should really do something with these. They're not going to grow if I don't plant them!" Therein lies the spiritual lesson.

The packet of unopened sunflower seeds is a metaphor for all the good we want to experience in our lives. I am not going to get to see any big, beautiful sunflowers outside my house if I don't do the work to plant, nurture, and cultivate those seeds. It is the same with the good thoughts that we think about our life. We have to put in the effort to live in alignment with Source, to know our Divine Truth, to believe our good is available to us, and to know and expect the best for our lives.

Act

Plant your seeds. Think good thoughts. Watch them bloom.

LIFE IN THE GARDEN
JULY 8

A friend once casually described Interfaith Ministry as, "the desire to study and experience all the flavors of God." This is a unique perspective that God could have many flavors. I liken it to having a diversified garden. Gardens that grow and flourish the best are ones that are not limited to one crop. Many varieties are planted, incorporating vegetables, herbs, flowers, native plants, etc. The garden becomes a healthy, balanced habitat. It creates a space for creativity, relaxation, beauty, harmony, and joy.

One could view various religions, spiritual traditions, and faiths in the same way, as different flavors of God. It's all the same God, same Spirit, same Source, just different flavors to be experienced and enjoyed. We use the flavor that works for us, the one we like, but it behooves us to live harmoniously in the garden of life next to all the other flavors.

Affirm

Today, I choose to celebrate the flourishing garden of all God's flavors!

"FIGHTING" FOR PEACE
JULY 9

You cannot fight for peace. It is counterintuitive and doesn't make any sense. The idea and energy of fighting for anything is like having a consciousness of war. To fight means to resist and be against. You can't be for peace while simultaneously resisting it and being against it. You can, however, *be* peace.

At the center of your being, you are peace. The divine quality of peace is your Truth. We have the opportunity to choose to show up as peace, to always be the presence of peace, wherever we are, at the grocery store, at our job, in our families, in our homes, walking down the street—anywhere. We can choose to be the presence of peace in our conscious awareness. So, let's do that! Let's cause the ripple effect of peace by allowing the principle of peace to express in us fully. Be peace, everywhere you go.

Affirm

I am peace. I choose to express as peace in the world.

EVERYTHING HAS CHANGED
JULY 10

Have you ever heard the saying, "You can never go home again"? I remember when I was a teenager and a young adult, I never understood it because I was very fortunate to have amazing parents who would always welcome me back home again, no matter what my situation was. The expression made no sense to me.

What that saying is really about is that you can never go home to the exact same scenario. For instance, if I grew up, went off to college, and then came home for the summer to my loving, welcoming parents, it would be different. I would no longer be a child living with my parents. I would be an adult coming home to visit temporarily. The circumstances change. Sure, you can still come home, but it means you can't come home to the exact same scenario and exact same way of experiencing your relationships.

This concept is similar to the Buddhist saying, "You can never step in the same river twice." Logically, of course, you can—you can even step in the same river from the same spot, but the river is not the same. The water is constantly flowing and moving. It is in flow. You're not stepping in that exact same "river." You are stepping into different flowing water, even though it goes by the name of the same river.

Life is always changing. We are always growing, aging, and becoming new versions of ourselves. We expand our understanding of life. You can never step in the same river twice, and you can't go home again. Life is all about change and how we handle it.

Ask

Who am I today? Who am I with regard to my spiritual understanding?

TAKE IN THE BEAUTY
JULY 11

Think about the most beautiful scene in nature you have ever experienced. Perhaps it was a waterfall, a river, the ocean, the Grand Canyon, mountains, or something else. How did you react while appreciating the scene? Maybe you gasped or smiled, shouted out "Wow!" or were speechless.

Yet, if you looked closely at that beautiful scene, you would likely find parts of it that would not be considered beautiful by human standards. A forest might be lush and breathtaking, but a closer look reveals tangled, exposed roots, fallen branches, and decaying leaves. A beach might seem stunning at sunset, but it could also be scattered with smelly seaweed, broken shells, and rotting driftwood. Nature is never perfectly polished, but we don't question its beauty. The broken, messy, unfinished parts are simply part of the whole. The same is true for us. As humans, we tend to focus on what seems flawed, wounded, or undeveloped, believing these parts disqualify us from being beautiful. Just like in nature, our beauty is found in the whole.

Natural beauty is a trait of the Divine. It is everywhere. Beauty expresses in you, through you, and as you. Life is beautiful, just because it is life. You are beautiful, just because you exist. You are Divine Beauty in expression.

Affirm

I am beautiful.
(Let the Truth of this affirmation sink in.)

A PRAYER FOR LOVE
JULY 12

Pray

There is only One Power, One Presence, One Life. It doesn't matter what we call this One Power—whether we call it God, Spirit, Universe, Source—this One Power simply <u>IS</u>. It is good and only good. It is Divine Love in expression. I know I live, and move, and have my being in this Power, in this Presence of Love. Therefore, I am an expression of Divine Love. This is my Truth. It is true for me, and it is true for everyone, including you. I know the Truth that Divine Love is who and what I am at the center of my being. At my very core, I am spiritually perfect.

Right here and now I release any negative patterns of thought and false beliefs that could possibly oppose this because nothing can oppose this Truth. All my negative thoughts and false beliefs dissolve away with these words. I know that this translates to loving, harmonious relationships, to feeling loved, to knowing the unconditional Love of the Divine. This is what I say yes to. This is what I give great thanks for. I give great thanks that love is what is real. I am grateful that Divine Love is who I am and at any moment I can remember to stand in this Truth. I see and recognize love all around me and in me.

I let this prayer go, knowing that it is being acted upon by Spiritual Law. I fully anticipate and expect this prayer to unfold in my life experience. I say yes to love and to being an expression of love in the world.

And So It Is. Amen.

THE DIRTY WATER OF CONSCIOUSNESS
JULY 13

Consider again the idea that a glass of dirty water can be a metaphor for your spiritual life. The dirt represents all our human muck, our negative thoughts, our problems, all the human ego stuff. It muddies up our clear consciousness. It makes it hard to remember the Truth of who we are. So, if you have a glass of dirty water, how do you get it clear?

An earlier entry suggested putting the glass down and leaving it alone. Let it be still. When the water gets still, all the muck sinks to the bottom of the glass. Everything from the bottom up gets clear. The muck is still there, but the water eventually becomes clear. For our spiritual life, that can look like our spiritual practice—maybe meditation, sitting in stillness, or prayer. It can be taking moments to be quiet to know our spiritual Truth. That makes the "water" of our consciousness become clear.

Another way to clear a glass of dirty water is to put the glass under a faucet until it is clear. Clean water comes out of the faucet, pushing out and replacing the dirty water. Spiritually, that could look like studying spiritual wisdom texts, reading inspirational books, taking spiritual classes, listening to and watching inspiring speakers perhaps at a spiritual center or church, having like-minded friends to support you, etc. Doing these things puts the Truth of who you are into your mind, clearing your consciousness.

Ask

How do I want to clear the dirty water of my consciousness?

DISCOMFORT IS GOOD
JULY 14

Sometimes discomfort is a great life motivator. It is in those moments when we feel the most uncomfortable that we have the opportunity to stop and say, "Hmm… maybe this is not where I'm supposed to be in my life. Maybe this is not the person I'm supposed to be with. Maybe this is not the job for me. Maybe this is not what I'm supposed to be experiencing." Pausing to consider what we do want to create for our lives—what we do want to experience—gives us clarity. Discomfort is not necessarily a bad thing.

An example of this is a person being diagnosed with an illness or disease, which is surely something that would cause discomfort. But what if the experience causes the person to change their habits and start a journey to manifest the return of health and wholeness? The discomfort can be a positive motivator that initiates good changes for them. Discomfort can be our teacher—showing us what we do want in life—if we are willing to see it that way.

Affirm

Discomfort is a tool that helps me create my best life.

ALL IS PERFECT
JULY 15

New Thought philosophy does not teach the concept of duality (e.g., opposing principles of good and evil) because the truth is that nothing can oppose God. There is only One Mind, One Consciousness, One Life. Within the realm of this Oneness, all is perfect. That sounds like incorrect grammar because *all* implies plural, but there is only one, and it is ALL—everything and everyone. All is perfect, simply by existing.

Human beings are always quick to point out flaws, imperfections, and failings, but the truth is, there is no spectrum of perfection and imperfection. This duality is made up in our minds. Spiritually, all is perfect, and this includes the divine expression that is you.

Affirm

I am perfect because I exist!

IS IT REALLY HARD?
JULY 16

A friend was trying to break into an industry that is very competitive and challenging. She had applied for a particular position with a company a few years earlier and was declined. After applying again, she was given an interview. After the interview, she was told that she was again not chosen for the position. While she was processing her feelings of sadness and unworthiness, I noticed she kept using similar words about this industry. She said things like, "It's so hard to get in with this industry. It's so challenging. It's too competitive."

The spiritual practitioner in me immediately noticed that those statements are all beliefs she holds. It is her choice to hold those beliefs while applying for jobs in that industry. The truth is that *someone* got chosen for that position. They certainly may have been more qualified or had more experience, but they also might have believed it was easy to get on in the industry. You can apply this to anything that seems hard and challenging. We get to choose what we believe.

Most people would say it is hard to get into medical school. Yet, people do it all the time. It is challenging to pass the BAR exam as an attorney. People do it all the time. It is hard to run a political campaign and get elected to office—people do it all the time.

Ask

Someone is doing the thing I believe is hard.
Is it hard, or are my beliefs preventing me from doing it?

TAKE A MOMENT
JULY 17

Whatever it is, it can wait.
You deserve a moment of stillness.
Your mind, body, and soul deserve your attention.
Give them your awareness.
You are worthy of your own self-love.
Whatever it is, let it go. Let it wait.

Affirm

I take this moment to be still and know that I am divine.

O.D.A.A.T
JULY 18

One of the slogans of Alcoholics Anonymous is "One day at a time." It encourages participants to focus solely on the present moment. You will sometimes hear an alcoholic declare, "I'm not going to drink today!" meaning, they are vowing their sobriety for the current day, not giving thought to anything beyond. Recovery can seem daunting and overwhelming, but concentrating on just one 24-hour period at a time makes the concept easier to manage.

This is true for many things in life. The present moment is where our power lies, and it is always *now*. Our awareness of *now* is all it takes to create powerful changes in our lives, and it is how we successfully manage our transformation, bit by bit, one day at a time, one hour at a time, one moment at a time.

Affirm

I am aware of how powerful I am in this present moment.

WHAT DO YOU WANT INSTEAD?
JULY 19

Let's imagine that you are experiencing a situation or problem you really want to change. You're not sure where to begin. You're not even sure how to pray about it. Here is a spiritual tip: Ask yourself, what is the divine quality, trait, or characteristic that you are wanting to experience, feel, and have instead of the problem? Whatever the problem, issue, or circumstance is, ignore it for a moment. Instead, think about what quality of the Divine you want to experience.

Divine qualities are our qualities—traits like Love, Peace, Harmony, Joy, Unity, Abundance, Prosperity, Intelligence, Creativity, Health, Wholeness, etc. These are divine qualities that we express as. What is it that you need to remind yourself is true? You may not be feeling it or seeing it, but that divine trait is what you need to focus on and remember because it *is* true for you. When you affirm it and get in alignment with this Truth, that's when you see it unfold in your experience.

Ask

*What is the divine quality, trait,
or characteristic that I want to experience today?*

POSITIVE SELF-TALK
JULY 20

We all have off-days regarding our appearance—days when maybe we aren't feeling quite as handsome, beautiful, and attractive as we would like. Perhaps your hair won't lie right, your makeup is messed up, or the cut of your shirt suddenly seems to make your stomach stick out. Do you slip into negative self-talk when that kind of day sneaks up on you? It is easy to do.

Have you ever looked in the mirror and mentally called yourself unattractive? Even worse, have you muttered under your breath and called yourself a name? Even in jest? Negative self-talk happens; we're human. I once said out loud to myself in the mirror, "I look like a scum bucket." I wasn't being serious, but I did immediately realize it was a ridiculous thing to say. The goal is to catch the negative self-talk, recognize that it is not the truth, and turn it around into a positive thought. I laughed, looked directly at myself again, and said, "Not true. The Truth is, I am expressing as the Beauty of the Divine!" This is true of you, as well.

Act

Look at yourself in the mirror and affirm:
"I am expressing as the Beauty of the Divine!"

PRAYER WORKS
JULY 21

Affirmative Prayer, also called Spiritual Mind Treatment, is a type of prayer that involves realizing that the good we want to see already exists in the One Mind of God. It must, for God is all—all that is visible and invisible. The Omnipresence of God is recognized and accepted—that is the prayer. There is no beseeching, begging, or declaring of lack. The unity of an individual with God is recognized. There is no asking to receive something from a version of God that is somehow separate from us.

This is a scientific manner of prayer based on universal Spiritual Laws about how the mind works, the way energy flows, cause and effect, and the interconnectedness of all life. When praying a Spiritual Mind Treatment, we see the perfection of God wherever a problem seems to be. Spiritual Law responds to our belief in that perfection, bringing about the good we desire.

Anyone with faith who understands these principles can get results. If you are struggling to see a demonstration of your prayer, or if you are in need of healing, a licensed spiritual practitioner trained in these principles can help. These practitioners and healers can be found at your local Centers for Spiritual Living, Unity, or Divine Science churches.

Affirm

Prayer works, and there is always help available to me.

SPIRITUALITY 24/7
JULY 22

For centuries, church has been a place where people gathered to worship on Sunday mornings. Week after week, they sat in pews, sang hymns, and listened to a long talk from a minister. While there is nothing wrong with this church model, over time, church attendance numbers have decreased. When the COVID-19 pandemic forced everyone to stay home, church services moved online, and members tuned in and watched via the internet. When social distancing restrictions ended, a lot of people realized for perhaps the first time that they didn't have to go back to a building once a week to receive spiritual instruction and guidance.

Increasingly, people are realizing that they can learn spiritual principles and develop their own spiritual practice. With the rise of social media, there are many platforms, accounts, and places you can go to for spiritual inspiration. Seeking out inspiration can be done individually, on any day of the week, at any time of day. Short snippets of sacred material throughout the day can uplift, encourage, and motivate.

This new way of "doing spirituality" is influencing the collective consciousness in a positive way. A shift is happening. One might say an awakening is taking place, as more people realize they can explore, study, and practice spirituality for themselves. You are powerful. You are divine. You are connected. You can pray, meditate, read books, and connect with your tribe in whatever way you wish, far beyond one hour on a Sunday morning.

Affirm

I am powerful, I am divine, and I am connected.

A PRAYER FOR SUCCESS
JULY 23

Pray

Knowing that I am one with the Power that made me, I trust that everything I could possibly need to accomplish, succeed, and achieve is already within me. God's great plan for the expansion of goodness in my life is my plan. It flows to me and operates in me. The recognition of God's Infinite Power within me ensures my success. I am always willing to see Divine Intelligence and Order in my life. I am open to the opportunities and lessons that appear on my path, saying yes to it all. I give great thanks for the Creative Process, knowing I am always empowered by the Infinite Intelligence of God. I am so grateful for all the ways I thrive—mentally, physically, emotionally, spiritually, and financially. I let this prayer go, joyfully anticipating and expecting demonstration of its fulfillment.

And So It Is. Amen.

HEARTBEAT PRESENT MOMENT
JULY 24

Think about every human being who is alive on the planet at this very moment. What do we all have in common? Many things, but for one, everyone has a beating heart within them. If you put your fingers on your wrist, you feel your pulse, your heartbeat, one after the other, *boom, boom, boom,* each beat marking another moment of your life. This is the present moment. Notice it. Your heartbeat is telling you that you are alive.

When you zero in on the reality of the current moment, you realize that this is the only moment anything truly happens. Your heart is beating, you are alive, and this is *now*. Everything that happens, happens in the present moment. Nothing happens in the past or in the future, only in the now. Life happens in the now; it is our moment of realization. The Power of God, life force energy, is active in you right now, with every beat of your heart. This is true for every beating heart. The present moment is always an opportunity for limitless possibilities.

Ask

What is happening for me right now?

JUDGE NOT
JULY 25

Judgment is an unfortunate part of many spiritual traditions. Several churches teach that God condemns the wicked, the sinful, and the proud. Worse, some churches believe we can be condemned to some version of hell, punished for our mistakes and transgressions. When we understand that there can be no separation, that we are one with a loving God and express as God's divine nature, that the only sin is believing we are separate from God, we come to realize that God cannot and does not condemn. There is no judgment.

(This is not to suggest we have a "free for all" opportunity to hurt people, have no morals, and live unethically. Karmically, cause and effect are real.) Ask this pertinent question.

Ask

If God does not judge, why do I judge myself?

Affirm

*I am free to love myself as much as God loves me.
This is the foundation of my life.*

BE LIKE COFFEE
JULY 26

If you take a pot of boiling water and put a potato in it, it is eventually going to soften the potato. If you put an egg in a pot of boiling water, it is going to harden the egg after a few minutes. When you slowly pour boiling water over coffee grinds, it makes coffee. These are three completely different responses to the same thing: boiling water. The water is a metaphor for life's problems and the difficult situations we deal with. Those situations can soften us and make us feel weak; they can harden us and make us mean; or they can change and transform us into something new and wonderful (like coffee).

How are you responding to life's difficulties? We can all respond in different ways to the same problem. The goal is to become like coffee. Use your spiritual practice, study spiritual principles, and embrace the Truth of your oneness and unity with the Divine. With this as the basis, if problems arise, we can allow ourselves to be transformed into something positive, with great purpose.

Ask

What's boiling in my life right now?
How am I allowing myself to respond?

RELEASING FEAR
JULY 27

Fear causes a lot of problems, especially in our physical bodies, our relationships, our work, and our prosperity. Releasing fear is a necessary step to live more in alignment with our divine nature and experience the good that is available to us.

Mindfulness questions are an effective way to identify, deny, process, and release fears. When afraid, ask yourself:

- *What, specifically, am I afraid of?* Naming our fears helps us more effectively deny them.
- *Can I think differently about this situation?* Perhaps there is another, more positive way to view the situation.
- *Who am I without this fear?* Without the emotion of fear, we can more easily remember the Truth of who we are as children of the Divine.
- *What is this fear trying to teach me?* There is often a lesson in our fears. We learn it by considering what it could be.
- *What steps can I take to feel better?* Deliberately choosing to do things that make us feel better raises our vibration and puts us more in alignment with God.
- *Will anything change if I continue to worry about this situation?* The answer is always no. This question shows us that our fear has no purpose. It has no value and no power. It helps us see the nothingness that fear is.

Affirm

*I choose today to release my fear and
remember the true power of God's Love.*

THINK ABOUT YOUR THINKING
JULY 28

Many of the difficulties we try to solve in life are not rooted in circumstance, but in the way we are thinking about them. We usually try to fix a problem by focusing on the problem itself instead of noticing how we are thinking about it. Addressing our thinking first is a more effective place to begin. The trouble with our thoughts is we often don't notice them enough to realize they need fixing! Consider how you are thinking about problems you might be experiencing.

> *How do you talk to yourself about it?*
> *How do you describe the situation to other people?*
> *Do you embellish, overdramatize, and complain?*
> *How do you frame the problem in your mind?*

That's what needs fixing. You may not believe that your thinking could possibly be the root of the problems you experience. But if it is, what do you have to lose by being willing to change your outlook?

Ask

> *What if the problem is a lesson that turns into a blessing?*
> *What if the situation is leading me to a new opportunity?*
> *What if it is easier than I think*
> *to change my attitude about the situation?*

DIVINE PRESENCE MEDITATION
JULY 29

Sit quietly in a comfortable position and allow your body to relax. Notice your breathing. As you breathe in, think of your breath as the One Life of Spirit, filling you and animating your being. As you exhale, focus on a sense of gratitude for your life. Do this several times. Breathe in the One Life of Spirit… breathe out gratitude for your life expression.

If thoughts arise, just notice them. Then, bring your attention back to your breath—the One Life of Spirit that is present within you. Take this moment to say to your higher self: "Help me shift my attention to the Divine Presence within me." Be open to experiencing whatever comes up for you—a feeling, a thought, an emotion, or sensation. Allow Spirit to make itself known within you.

Mentally invite this connection to stay with you. Set the intention to be aware of this Presence throughout the day. Tell yourself it is easy to be aware of this Presence. Decide to make a note of when you see it, feel it, sense it, hear it, and know it.

Affirm

I am aware of the Divine Presence within me all day long.

BE AT EASE
JULY 30

Are you holding tension in your body? Do a quick scan right now and check. How are your eyes? Are you squinting at the page and furrowing your brow without realizing it? How is your jaw? Make sure it is loose and relaxed. Check your posture and your shoulders. Roll them back and see if you can pull them down and away from your ears. How is your stomach? Are you holding it in? How do your hips and lower back feel? Imagine any tension being released. Point and flex your feet. Circle your ankles; then allow them to soften. Check in, release, and relax. Take a deep breath in and exhale slowly. In this moment, place your awareness on your body's ability to relax and be at ease.

The Latin prefix *dis* means "a negative, reversing force." Therefore, the word *disease*, broken down, means not-at-ease, or the reverse of being at ease (dis-ease). You are spiritually perfect, and your physical body has within it the ability to express as perfect wholeness. Be at ease in this moment. Feel the wholeness that is your divine nature.

Affirm

All is well. I am perfect, whole, and complete. I choose to live at ease.

THE PLACEBO EFFECT AND HEALING
JULY 31

The placebo effect is a fascinating concept because it challenges the truth of how we heal. Instead of medicine, a patient is given a sugar pill or a saline injection. Those patients often report improvements in their health, to a similar degree to the patients who received actual medicine. The idea is that people believe so strongly in the "fake" treatment that they begin to heal themselves.

Studies have shown that, even in cases when patients were told they were being given a placebo, healing still took place. Healing occurred because the people believed so much in the treatment's healing power that it just didn't matter that the medication wasn't real. This demonstrates the power of the subconscious mind. Patients were able to heal themselves because their subconscious minds were conditioned to put their belief in some "thing" external from them, like a pill or injection.

How often in your childhood did you feel sick and were taken to the doctor? The doctor prescribed you a pill, a cough syrup, or gave you a shot to make you better. We've all experienced this scenario our whole life. We are programmed to think that pills, medicine, shots, etc. heal. But do they?*

Ask

What if I changed my belief from giving power to something outside of me to heal, to placing my belief in the power inside of me to heal myself?
Is it possible my healing is simply a matter of belief?
What do I believe about my healing? Who heals me? What heals me?

---

* The author encourages readers to seek appropriate medical advice and/or treatment. The ideas presented here are intended to compliment, not replace, professional medical care.

AUGUST

THINK WELL OF THEM
AUGUST 1

Do you have someone in your life who is constantly having problems and going through drama, but they are not interested in spiritual solutions? They don't want to hear about how spiritual practices and spiritual principles could help them. They don't want to dive into their thoughts and beliefs or know the Truth about who they are as a child of the Divine. So, what do you do? How can you best help?

When this happens, remember you can always work on your own consciousness. Watch the way you think and talk about the person. For example, a friend of mine asked me about a family member who had been experiencing a lot of problems recently. I had to catch myself in how I answered and make a conscious choice in how I spoke about the situation. We always have the opportunity to think and speak well of someone, to know the Truth for them. Are they experiencing a bunch of drama and problems? Sure. But is that their Truth? No. Their Divine Truth is that they are healthy, whole, complete. They are loved, supported, and surrounded by the harmony of all Life.

Knowing there is only One Consciousness, God's Consciousness, my thoughts and beliefs can help play a role in other people's problems resolving themselves. We can still know the Truth of a positive outcome and a peaceful resolution, even if the other person doesn't want to hear the truth and do this for themselves.

Affirm

I speak and think of only good. I stay aligned with God.

ANGER IN THE BODY
AUGUST 2

When you experience the emotion of anger, you hold it in your physical body, whether you realize it or not. If you hold on to anger for an extended period of time, it can turn into disease and illness. Anger is the number one emotion that causes dis-ease. Use this opportunity to check in with yourself.

Ask

Am I angry about anything in my life?
Am I angry about something in the past that I thought I had moved on from, but maybe I actually haven't?
Do I have some forgiving to do?
Is there some situation or pain that needs to be processed or released?

Act

You are never powerless over your anger;
there are many practices and exercises
you can do that clear repressed, trapped emotions.
Consider forgiveness exercises, journaling, and visualizing.
Talk with a therapist or spiritual practitioner.
Write down what you are angry about on paper
and then burn it safely or tear it up.
Do the work to release your anger,
for the good of your human body experience.
Remember, there is no anger in God,
only peace, wholeness, and love.

BREATHE LIKE THIS…
AUGUST 3

Breathwork has long been associated with sharpening your focus, lowering your stress levels, and helping your body relax, often as part of a meditation practice. One specific breathwork exercise is "alternate nostril breathing." It involves isolating each nostril by breathing in one and exhaling out the other.

It would look like this: Close your right nostril with your thumb. Breathe in deeply through your left nostril. Close both nostrils and hold your breath for a beat or two. Keep your left nostril closed, open your right nostril, and exhale slowly.

Repeat the cycle, closing your left nostril, breathing in through your right nostril. Close both and hold your breath a moment. Open your left nostril and exhale slowly. Repeat the whole process again. Doing this breathwork for five minutes a day reaps the benefits of increased focus, a slower heart rate, balanced energy, reduced stress, and an overall sense of relaxation. It is a wonderful way to begin your meditation practice.

Affirm

I use my breath as a tool to slow down, focus, and relax.

POSSIBILITY CONSCIOUSNESS
AUGUST 4

Possibility is a state of awareness. Most children live in a state of possibility consciousness, believing that anything is possible—anything they imagine can exist and happen. An adult might think this kind of thought process is nonsensical, but fantasy, dreaming, imagining, etc., are all normal parts of childhood belief and play. We are told in the Bible that we are to "become like little children" to enter the kingdom of heaven. We know this is metaphorical. To enter the kingdom of heaven (the consciousness of all our good being available to us in manifest form) we have to believe like a child. We access our good by thinking in possibility consciousness. Childlike belief in our dreams and fantasies, where anything is possible, is what creates them in manifest form.

Ask

What is possible for my life?
What do I believe is possible?
What can I daydream about and imagine today?

GOD'S CONSCIOUSNESS IS OURS
AUGUST 5

There is only One Consciousness, and it is God's Consciousness. It is also ours. We can apply this awareness to all aspects of life, if we choose to use our free will to do so. We can choose to see peace where there is war. Prosperity where there is lack. Love where there is hate. Wholeness where there is disease. Order where there is chaos, and on and on. God never worries and frets over human situations like fighting with a neighbor, having to pay bills, dealing with sickness, or feeling overwhelmed by life, but we sure do!

If we have a problem, it is only our viewpoint of the problem that interferes with the solution we wish to see. Spirit never has a problem; it has only solutions and perfection. It may seem unrealistic that life could be this simple, but what if it is? The Infinite Intelligence of all life is ours to experience, be aware of, and enjoy. One Life, One Consciousness. This is the mindset. This is the way of life. Let it be simple, and let it be so.

Affirm

God's Consciousness is my consciousness.

LITTLE WORDS, BIG MEANING
AUGUST 6

I AM is the name of God. It is our point of access to the power of God; we use the "I AM" to create whatever possibility we want to experience. In Genesis 4, there is a line that in the past was translated as, "Men began to call upon the name of the Lord," as if people were begging and beseeching help from a God that lived outside of them. This translation teaches duality and separation, which we know is false.

In modern times, that passage has been correctly translated as, "Men began to call *themselves* by the name of the Lord." That is a totally different statement. People became aware of the living Spirit, the Light of God within, which we call into existence by speaking "I AM." By calling ourselves the name of God we claim our oneness with the Creative Process. By paying attention to what follows our "I AM," we use the power of God to create whatever possibility we desire. This is why it is so important to speak well of your life, affirming good things that are in alignment with your spiritual Truth.

Ask

What good thing can I declare today?

Affirm

I am perfect, whole, and complete because I am divine.

NEW THOUGHT OR NEW AGE?
AUGUST 7

New Thought is an umbrella term for spiritual philosophies that emerged in the early 19th century, emphasizing metaphysics and the creative power of thought. *The Science of Mind*® was originally written in 1926, but prior to that, Divine Science emerged in the 1880s. Unity Church was founded in 1889. Based on ancient spiritual traditions, New Thought philosophy draws wisdom from Greek philosophy, Hinduism, Buddhism, and, of course, the teachings of Jesus.

I share this because *New Thought* is often confused with *New Age*. While there can be overlap, they are not the same. *New Age* refers to a broader cultural movement that gained traction in the late 20th century and includes a wide range of approaches to spirituality, health, and conscious living. Its meaning shifts depending on who is using the term, which can make it difficult to define clearly.

The deeper question is, do these labels really matter?

Just as the Divine has been named in countless ways across time and cultures, our beliefs and practices are called many things, too. Language is a human construct—a way for us to point toward something far greater than words can ever define. What matters is not what we call a philosophy, a practice, or even God, but the intention behind it and how it shows up in our lives.

Affirm

*My spiritual journey is not measured by terminology.
It is revealed through my choices, my growth,
and the way I live what I believe.*

ASK THIS, NOT THAT
AUGUST 8

Here is a great way to shift your consciousness immediately, especially when you are experiencing a problem. Instead of saying, "Why is this happening to me?" ask, "What is this trying to teach me?" Compare those two different thoughts. How often do we experience something negative that makes us frustrated or scared? We get upset, wring our hands, feel like a victim, and cry out, "Why is this happening to me?" This is a normal human response to difficulties.

But we can also learn something new, an alternative way to respond, and say instead, "What is this trying to teach me?" This question creates a shift in your consciousness that feels empowering instead of powerless. "Why is this happening to me?" feels like there is an outside force separate from you doing this to you, but that is not true. You are very powerful. When you stop and ask the Spirit within what this situation is teaching you, you can then learn from it, move forward, and elevate your consciousness.

Affirm

I am willing to observe, learn, and grow.

WHAT'S INSIDE?
AUGUST 9

To make freshly squeezed orange juice, you do exactly that—squeeze the orange until the juice comes out. We expect orange juice to come out of the orange, not lemon juice, or cranberry juice, or anything else. Orange juice comes out because that is what's inside the orange. This is a great metaphor for human beings.

When we are stressed, feeling the pressure of life, it is as if we are being "squeezed." We feel pressure in our relationships and our work. We can even feel squeezed by our health experiences, forced to pay attention to them. What comes out of us in these kinds of moments when we feel squeezed?

Sometimes anger can come out, or fear, hatred, and bitterness. We get to choose what comes out of us in these moments. Love is inside you. At the center of your being, love is who and what you are.

Ask

Is love coming out of me when I am squeezed?

REMEMBER TO REST
AUGUST 10

Sometimes we get frustrated when unexpected illness and symptoms have us laid up in bed to recover. But what if we change our perspective? Instead of saying, "I have to rest," what if you said, "I *get* to rest. I am *able* to rest and recover." As humans, rest is vital for us. We use our bodies, and they serve us well. But sometimes, we end up with symptoms, illness, or dis-ease, and those things tell us we are perhaps not resting enough, not living in ease, not living in the flow of our divine nature. Rest is an honor, a privilege, and a responsibility. It's a good part of recovery and healing, and a good part of life!

Affirm

I give myself permission to rest.

SURRENDERING
AUGUST 11

Sometimes it feels as though nothing we do improves our situation. The disease spreads. Divorce papers are signed. The house goes into foreclosure. Someone else got the job we wanted. The car is totaled. Our last dollar is spent.

We feel frustrated. Scared. Overwhelmed. None of this is what we chose!

The Lord's prayer in the Bible says, "Thy will be done," not ours. We dig our heels in and shout, "But I have free will! My thoughts and beliefs are powerful!" This is true.

However, surrendering to Divine Will can be an important part of our spiritual journey.

There is no God in the sky, floating on a cloud, arbitrarily throwing problems and challenges at us. We do not surrender to a power that is separate from us. We do not give up and admit we are powerless. On the contrary, surrendering is a powerful choice. Surrendering simply means trusting that there is a higher perspective that we may not understand. It means knowing that the Spirit of Life within us does understand. Surrendering means choosing to trust Life and letting it flow.

Affirm

I surrender my fears and worries to the Divine.

LOVING THIS BODY
AUGUST 12

We all experience physical challenges at some point. Have you ever met a person who has never experienced a day of sickness, injury, or pain? One of the drawbacks of being human (if you see it as a drawback) is that the human body doesn't last forever. They tend to break down after a while. We can accelerate this breakdown with all sorts of unhealthy choices, or we can perhaps slow it down with better, healthier ones. But, even if we aggressively prioritized our physical wellness, making extremely healthy choices for our entire life, the aging process would still eventually catch up with us. So, what is the point of being here if our human bodies ultimately fall apart and fail?

Does your body have a spiritual purpose? Yes. Your body holds and expresses your spirit while you are here on the planet. Your spirit is eternal, invisible, and divine, and it is held somewhere inside this temporary human vessel. You can bet if God is expressing in you, through you, and as you, then your body is wholly and unconditionally loved.

We can't fathom how much we are loved. Go beyond the greatest human love you have ever felt—beyond love for parent, spouse, child, or pet. Turn it all inward to your body. Love every organ, muscle, cell, hair follicle, and toenail. Love the job your body does, housing your true spiritual self.

Ask

Can I love my body as much as God does?

IT'S THE FEAR
AUGUST 13

How do you get rid of a problem? What is it that needs healing? From a spiritual perspective, it is good to consider whether it is the actual problem or the fear associated with the problem that needs healing. When we boil it down, getting rid of the fear would heal the problem. What are problems but the outpicturing of fear in our lives? Our troubles are often nothing but our fears made manifest.

Ask yourself: "What do I trust more in, my fear, or my perfect wholeness in God?" When working to heal our fear, we must counteract, offset, and replace the fear with our solid faith in God. How do we do that? By absorbing as much spiritual Truth as possible until the fear is negated. Speak it, think it, walk in it, and believe it.

Affirm

I have nothing to fear but fear.
Today, I walk in confidence, knowing my faith is strong.

HOW ARE WE TO ASK?
AUGUST 14

Let us consider the topic of prayer. The minute we ask God for something (whether it be healing, abundance, help with a relationship, or a job, etc.), the moment we ask for it is the moment we admit the lack of the thing. We only ask for something when we believe we don't have it. God, Spirit, Universe, Source doesn't understand anything about lack. How could It, when God is total and complete abundance of all good?

Consider the Bible scripture that tells us to "ask, believing you will receive" (Matt. 21:22). From a New Thought perspective, the believing is more important than the asking. We have to ask in a way that we believe we have already received what we wanted. This is what puts Spiritual Law in motion and brings your desire to manifestation. This is a unique way to pray, to pray in a way that you convince yourself you have already received the thing you are praying for. This, in essence, is Affirmative Prayer and Spiritual Mind Treatment.

Affirm

The key to my prayer is the believing.

PICK OUT THE VOICE
AUGUST 15

When you listen to a symphony, try to pick out the individual instruments that are being played. It takes deep, focused listening, concentration, and lots of practice. This is true for our spiritual practice as well. There are voices all around us, bombarding us with information, distractions, and noise. It can be challenging to tune out all the other voices chattering over the small voice of the Divine that is within you.

Whatever you are hearing, whoever is talking to you or at you, whatever chaos may be swirling around you, allow yourself to be still. Use your spiritual practice: prayer, meditation, study, stillness, etc. This is how we learn to pick out and recognize what is already within us—our divine nature and spiritual Truth.

Affirm

Today, I listen to the still, small voice within me.

YOUR GREAT GOOD
AUGUST 16

We know God to be good and only good. We also know that God is omnipresent—present always, in all ways. That means your good, which is synonymous with God, is always here. There is no excuse, condition, or circumstance that can possibly separate you from the infinite supply of resources available to you. You cannot be excluded from the abundance of this world.

Once you recognize abundance as a divine trait and prosperity as a naturally occurring part of life, the next thing is to work on your receptivity. You are a part of this abundant life; it operates in you, through you, as you. It is your birthright to share in the great bounty of Life and experience it fully. Choose to believe in and accept the great good that is available to you.

Affirm

I am always seeing good opportunities for my prosperity.
I am open and ready to receive the abundance that is rightfully mine.

LOVE IT ALL
AUGUST 17

A tenet of New Thought philosophy is the idea that we are each, individually, perfect, whole, and complete in God. Does this leave room for imperfections? Not really! The Truth is, we are perfect (spiritually, at least). But how many of us believe we are physically perfect? For instance, if someone asked you, "What do you consider your biggest physical flaw?" would you have an answer? Most people would.

From a wholeness perspective, we would love all of ourselves, even the parts that we deem flawed or imperfect. Yes, I'm talking about physical imperfections: the bald spots, double chins, sagging bellies, skin blemishes, or even our crooked, hairy toes, but also our general weaknesses—the things we think we just aren't good at.

When we do the work to recognize and love our own imperfections (and make no mistake, it *is* work), the natural consequence of that is that it helps us recognize and love the things we find imperfect in others. Doing this directs us to toward the Truth of our oneness and unity.

Affirm

I am the Wholeness of the Divine.
Understanding this means loving all of myself.
Loving all of myself helps me love all others.

ARE THEY STILL HERE?
AUGUST 18

The message of eternal life is part of most, if not all, religions. While this can be comforting to think about when we lose people we love, it is still hard to understand. If we believe our loved ones live on, where do they live? In what form? How can we hear from them and know that this is true? As with everything in life, what we believe plays an important role in what we can experience.

You either believe in the possibility that life is eternal, or you don't. What if the more you believe in eternal life, the more signs of eternal life you see? In other words, the more you believe your loved ones in spirit are still with you, communicating with you, and sending you signs, the more you see their signs and sense their communication. How would one go about proving this concept? Spiritual healers, mystics, psychics, and mediums are interesting resources, but this concept is something you may have to investigate on your own to prove or disprove for yourself.

What do you have to lose? Talk about your loved ones in spirit. Think about them, talk to them, and communicate with them. Expect to receive signs from them. When we walk confidently with the expectation of experiencing all of life—this side of the veil and the spiritual side of the veil—we are more likely to receive the wisdom, clarity, and love we are seeking.

Affirm

I know that life does not end and love never dies.

ALWAYS AT CHOICE
AUGUST 19

What if you choose to think about something other than your problem? In fact, what if you chose to think the opposite of your problem? God has no problems. What is the Truth in God that you can remind yourself about and immerse yourself in, instead of whatever problem you are experiencing?

Affirm

I am free to choose joy instead of pain.
I am free to choose gratitude instead of lack.
I am free to choose wholeness instead of illness.
I am free to choose peace instead of conflict.
I am free to choose the light of heaven over the darkness of the world.
I am free to choose how I want to live, think,
and show up in this world.

CLOSED FOR MAINTENANCE
AUGUST 20

I recently headed to my favorite drive-through coffee shop, intent on getting my favorite drink. I had the dog with me, since they always give her a dog treat. No one was waiting in line as I pulled up, which was excellent! Then, I discovered why. There was a paper taped to the window with a handwritten note: "Sorry, we are closed for maintenance today. Our espresso machines need some love. We appreciate our customers, and will be back open tomorrow, ready to bring you the best coffee!"

At first, I was so annoyed, and so was the dog—no treat for her! I had driven all the way there for nothing. But then I thought about the way they phrased the explanation. Those espresso machines work hard every day. Of course, they would need maintenance every now and then. Maintenance ensures the machines work efficiently and last a long time. The managers were responsible business owners.

The metaphor here, of course, is that we are, each of us, in the "business" of being human. We have bodies, minds, and spirits. This experience, this being a human, requires maintenance, and we need to be responsible about it. We require self-love and self-care. Don't ignore your maintenance. Take time to go within to serve your mind, body, and spirit in whatever way resonates with you.

Ask

Is it time to close for maintenance?

STAY AWARE THROUGH THE PAIN
AUGUST 21

Sometimes, we see the pain and suffering of our friends, acquaintances, or even strangers from across the globe, and we immediately feel sadness and sorrow. Our mood shifts. It brings us down to see such misery; we hate to see humanity hurting.

In these moments, it helps to remember that when we experience something we don't want, we begin to realize with certainty what it is we *do* want. When things look the most hopeless and distressing, it is the moment to remind yourself of great Truths and infinite possibilities. Sadness and darkness remind us how much humanity thrives in happiness. We remember how truly brilliant the light is.

When you see pain and suffering taking place, use it as a launching point for your spiritual awareness. Stand firm in your faith, knowing that love is real, the potential for peace exists, and a better world is possible.

Affirm

*Today, I let the pain and suffering of life
awaken me to the possibility of a better world.*

LET IT GO
AUGUST 22

The Bible is clear about the importance of forgiveness. We know we are to forgive others so that we may be forgiven. That means releasing any past hurts, holding no complaints, and having no judgment. It is always easier said than done. But the alternative haunts us, weighs us down, and clouds our consciousness. That is no way to live. Is there a new way to view forgiveness, to make it feel easier to do, more plausible?

One way of looking at it is, forgiveness is letting go of the hope that the past was different. When we are tightly holding on to the past, it is like arguing with reality. The past is never going to be different. Whatever happened, happened in the past. It is not happening now in the present moment. Choosing not to forgive the person, situation, or action is choosing to spoil the peace of this present moment. Only you know if it is within the realm of possibility to let go of the false hope that the past can be different. It is all up to you.

Affirm

I am letting go of the hope that the past was different.
In my willingness to forgive, I, too, am forgiven and set free.

A PRAYER FOR YOUR DESIRE
AUGUST 23

Think of something you want, a desire you would like to experience. Take this desire into your heart and mind. Shift your thought to a place of possibility, to where you believe you have already received this desire. Let's pray a simple Affirmative Prayer.

Pray

God is all there is, and God is good. I am one with God. Whatever the outcome and Truth I wish to experience, I claim it as my good right here and now. Knowing all things are possible and all possible good is available to me in this moment, I say yes to achieving, receiving, and accepting my desire. I am grateful for all the ways God's Truth unfolds in my experience. There is so much to be thankful for. I give great thanks for the way Spirit works. Good things are happening in my life. Releasing this prayer, I let it go, trusting and expecting its fulfillment.

And So It Is. Amen.

LOUSY DAYS HAPPEN
AUGUST 24

You can have a crappy day and still be spiritual. Ministers have crappy days. My work is centered on positive, inspiring, uplifting ideas, spiritual principles, spiritual practices, ways we can live in alignment with our true divine nature in order to draw our good to us and have the best possible life experience—and sometimes, I have crappy days. Days when I am in a funk. I might cry, complain to the people around me, think negative thoughts, and have negative self-talk. I might skip my meditation practice and forget to turn to prayer. I might skip my spiritual reading that would inspire my day. Why? Because I'm human.

So are you.

Today's message is to give yourself some grace the next time you are having a crappy day. It doesn't mean you are not spiritual. It doesn't mean you don't know your spiritual Truth. It doesn't mean you have rejected God. You are allowed to have a bad day now and then. You are allowed to occasionally forget your divinity.

A bad day doesn't change the fact that you are whole and complete in God, fully surrounded, supported, and loved. It doesn't change anything about God's perfection that is expressing in you, through you, and as you. The trick is to not stay stuck in your bad day forever. Eventually, come out of it, and circle back to your Truth.

Affirm

Today, I give myself grace. A bad day is always temporary.

ARE YOU AWARE?
AUGUST 25

A stranger once struck up a conversation with me about spirituality. He described his disdain for religion, insisting that too many wars were started and lives had been lost in the name of "God." He told me, "Religion has nothing to do with faith. Faith, I can get behind. It matters. Nobody needs religion." It was a bold statement that I understood.

As the number of people choosing to be "spiritual, but not religious" continues to rise, we see the faithful awakening to universal Truths. It is happening with or without religion. Maybe all the religions can crumble if it propels humanity to a higher collective consciousness. After all, the phoenix must burn to ashes if there is any hope of it being reborn into something better.

Humanity is discovering new choices for our faith. We are zooming out, widening our spiritual lenses, and seeing the universal Truth of our awareness for ourselves. We aren't just becoming aware; we are recognizing that we are *awareness itself*, which is bigger and better than any religion.

Ask

To what do I wish to be faithful?
A building? A book? A teaching? A being? A ritual?
A prophet? A leader?
Or maybe… The Unity of All Life? My Soul?
Spiritual Law? My divine nature?

What do I know to be true deep in my mind, body, and spirit?

WHO IS UNWORTHY?
AUGUST 26

Unworthiness is one of the most common emotional traumas people carry from their childhood. It only takes one flippant remark, an angry outburst, or an unexpectedly cruel moment of discipline to make a child feel devalued, worthless, and shamed. It doesn't mean we all had horribly abusive parents, though certainly some of us did. It means that, as grown adults, these unprocessed feelings of unworthiness can negatively impact our belief system.

From a spiritual perspective, unworthiness is simply not true. You cannot exist (be alive in a body, with a mind, as an eternal soul, expressing as the Divine) *and* be unworthy. Those things are mutually exclusive.

If you are here, you are worthy.
If you were unworthy, you could not be here.
That is how simple it is.

Our humanness, our human ego, can absolutely feel unworthy. That is why we do deep dives into spiritual wisdom, spiritual practice, meditation, prayer, affirmations, etc., to fill us with the Truth. We rewire our brain to our Divine Truth and know that because we are here we are worthy to express as the Divine.

Affirm

I am here, and I am worthy. Because I am alive, I am enough.

IT'S A MYSTERY
AUGUST 27

Have you seen glimpses of the great mystery of life? There are moments, however brief, where we take in the majesty and wonder of it all. Perhaps while staring up at the blanket of stars in the evening sky, listening to ocean waves gently crash to the shore, seeing the gentle rays of the sunrise spill over the horizon, seeing a tiny seedling make its way up from the soil, attending the birth of a baby and marveling at the instinctive natural process that unfolds.

What is the meaning of it all?

These moments are both precious and powerful. They give us a glimpse of the infinite nature of Life. It is an inexplicable mystery. You are a part of it. You are observing what already exists within you.

Affirm

I am not just a part of the mystery. I am the mystery.

CHANGE THE THOUGHT
AUGUST 28

Have you ever thought about where your feelings come from? What, within us, creates them? Our feelings are triggered and created from our thoughts. Your thoughts create your reality and the feelings you have about your reality.

If you are feeling something you don't want to feel, the first step is to notice it. Noticing feelings and emotions is a skill that takes practice. Once you notice the feeling, particularly if you are dealing with a situation you don't want to experience, the next step is to see if you can identify the thought behind it. How are you thinking about the condition? What do you believe about the situation? Can you think differently about it? It can be tremendously eye-opening to simply realize that a thought can be changed. Thoughts are malleable. Whatever is going on in life, whatever we're dealing with, our power lies in our thoughts about the thing. We are in control of our thoughts, and this makes us very powerful. It makes it so we can change and transform our lives.

Affirm

Whatever it is, I am only dealing with a thought.

JUST FIVE MINUTES
AUGUST 29

A dog trainer once explained that most people feel like they never have enough time in the day to really invest in training their dog. We all want a well-trained dog, but we don't want to do the work to get it! It feels like an overwhelming task, and we end up living with an untrained dog instead. The trainer pointed out that if you can spare just five minutes a day to commit to working with your dog, you will see improvement in your dog's behavior in a matter of days. Just that little bit of time—five minutes a day—can make a big difference over time.

This idea applies to anything we want to accomplish. If you spend just five minutes a day focused on your spirituality—on your relationship with the Divine—reading something inspirational, connecting with a like-minded spiritual friend, etc., you will see a positive impact in your life. Spending five minutes a day connecting with Source in whatever way you want is a form of self-care. It keeps you in balance and gives you a dedicated moment to check in with the Truth of who and what you are.

Act

You can spare five minutes a day.
Reading this entry took less than two.

SPREAD OUT YOUR SPIRITUALITY
AUGUST 30

An online fitness coach encourages people to move throughout the day. He challenges his viewers to do a particular movement 100 times a day. You don't have to do it all in one sitting, which would feel overwhelming, daunting, and potentially strenuous. You can spread it out, break it up, and do it throughout the day until you have reached 100. Short bursts of exercise are much more manageable and better for your body.

This reminds me of a homework assignment I had for a prosperity class. We were challenged to say the affirmation "I am prosperous" out loud 100 times a day. It, of course, seemed overwhelming and time-consuming. Who has time to sit there and chant an affirmation 100 times in a row? But we didn't have to do that; we had all day to get the affirmations completed, spreading them out however we wanted. We could do ten, in short bursts, ten times a day, or we could say twenty affirmations, five times a day.

You do the work on your consciousness, affirming the Truth of your prosperity and your abundance by spreading it out throughout the day. It makes a big impact in the same way little bursts of exercise throughout the day make a big impact on your physical fitness. Small bits of spirituality and exercise are more convenient and workable.

Ask

What if I combined physical exercises with affirmations?

FIND THE JOY
AUGUST 31

I once was on a very turbulent flight. The fasten seatbelt sign was on, beverage service suspended, and flight attendants were asked by the pilots to take their seats. I wasn't the only nervous passenger as the plane bounced and dipped. Audible gasps could be heard. Then I heard something else. From the seat directly behind me, a little girl's voice sang out. "Wheeeeee! This is FUN!" she squealed.

Laughter instantly broke the heavy moment. She innocently asked her mother why people were laughing at her. None of us was laughing at her—we were laughing at ourselves. Such a wonderful, joyful perspective she had! Children naturally seek and find joy in every moment. Maybe we were all silly to be afraid. I found myself wondering—could I possibly change my opinion of this moment? Could I stop focusing on fear and instead find the joy in it all?

I had a similar experience while walking my dog on the beach. A young boy was playing in the sand while his father watched nearby. He waved at me excitedly and said, "Hi!"

I waved back with a gentle smile.

He tipped his head to the side and looked at me, confused. "Aren't you having *fun*?" he demanded.

His father and I laughed. "Oh, yes!" I assured him, smiling broadly. I felt lighter and happier.

As if she knew what we were discussing, my dog jumped all around, pulled on her leash with her mouth, and acted silly. I laughed at her, too. Look to the kids and dogs. They always get it.

Act

Have fun. Find the joy.

SEPTEMBER

NOT THAT PERSON!
SEPTEMBER 1

Do you ever dread an interaction with someone? Perhaps you avoid a certain coworker when you see them coming down the hall because they talk too much. You notice a particular friend is calling, but you let it go to voicemail because the last time they called, all they did was complain. You try to avoid eye contact with your neighbor because you don't want to get caught in a conversation with them about politics again. We've all done things like this. We base our expectations on past experience. It is human nature to do so. What if we consciously changed our expectations? Anticipating different, better outcomes of these scenarios is what helps create them. Can you believe in the possibility that something better could happen the next time you encounter people like the ones described?

I once worked with a woman who drove me crazy. I found her to be quite bossy, even though we were colleagues at the same corporate level. I dreaded coming into work. But then, I began actively visualizing myself entering work joyfully, feeling happy to be there. I imagined pleasant interactions with the woman I worked with. I carried with me the expectation that she was in a great mood, easy to get along with, and focused on her own work. It wasn't long before my attitude about her changed completely, and working with her became much more agreeable.

Affirm

*I can always change my expectations
and anticipate a good outcome.*

ACKNOWLEDGING THE FEMININE
SEPTEMBER 2

The New Thought movement is one of the few spiritual traditions founded, influenced, and advanced by women. Surprisingly, it began at a time when women had very few rights as citizens. Emma Curtis Hopkins*, often credited as the founder of New Thought, created the Christian Science Theological Seminary in 1888 and became the first woman to ordain others as ministers. Many of her female students and students of her students went on to establish their own successful New Thought theological organizations, like Nona Brooks, Fannie James, and Malinda Cramer, who all started Divine Science, and Myrtle Fillmore, who co-founded Unity with her husband Charles.

Emma Curtis Hopkins taught social reformers, women's rights activists, suffragists, authors, poets, journalists, publishers, and teachers. New Thought philosophy is interfaith-based at its core, finding universal Truth in all religions. It is surprisingly progressive, seeing God as ALL—both Father and Mother. The feminine background of this teaching is worth acknowledging and honoring. We can choose to see the beauty in the whole of life by welcoming the contributions of all.

Affirm

I honor feminine wisdom and acknowledge the full expression of Divine Truth through all people in all forms.

---

* *Emma Curtis Hopkins was born on September 2, 1849.*

AS YOU LOVE YOURSELF
SEPTEMBER 3

When we consider the Bible message that the second greatest commandment is to, "Love your neighbor as yourself," (Matt. 22:39) most of us know what to do with it. We look outward and see what we can do for our neighbors. But the line says more than that. It says love your neighbor…as *yourself*. We are supposed to be loving our neighbors in the same way we love ourselves. What way is that?

Do you love yourself? Do you show compassion for yourself and give yourself grace when you make a mistake? Do you speak kindly to yourself? Sometimes we need to start there first before we look to our neighbors. Can you look yourself in the mirror and say out loud, "I love you! You matter, and I care about you." It can feel very strange to do this, but it is a powerful spiritual practice. Then, you can focus on loving your neighbor as you love yourself.

Affirm

Today, I love myself in the same way I love my neighbor.

IN THIS MOMENT
SEPTEMBER 4

Take these statements into a time of contemplation. Consider how they bring you into the present moment.

In this moment, I am alive.
In this moment, I am breathing.
In this moment, my heart is beating.
In this moment, I am safe.
In this moment, love is within me.
In this moment, peace is here.
In this moment, all is well.

Now, it is your turn.

Ask

In this moment,
what Truth is unfolding for me that I can contemplate?

A DAY OF SELF-CARE
SEPTEMBER 5

Self-care is self-love, and self-love is crucial to our health and well-being. Has it been a while since you've made yourself a priority? Use this reading as a reminder to love and care for yourself. What are you planning to do for self-care today? How do you plan to focus on loving the human expression you are choosing to show up as in the world? The options are endless.

Scheduling a routine doctor appointment is self-care. So is taking a bath or a long, hot shower. Making a dentist appointment or going to the hair salon or barber shop counts as self-care. Taking a walk in nature is also self-care. Planning a vacation, relaxing on the couch as you read, or taking a day off from work can be considered self-care, too. A meditation practice is self-care, as is consciously making the decision to speak kindly to yourself. What does the human version of your divine self need today? Take a moment to think about it and respond to yourself with love.

Affirm

I make choices today that love and support my human expression.

THINK OUTSIDE THE BOX
SEPTEMBER 6

You have heard, "Think outside the box." Consider its meaning, especially if you are dealing with a problem or situation that needs a creative solution. Thinking outside the box requires that we see from a new perspective, one that is not bound by limitations. Humans are not used to thinking in this way; we often feel limited, constricted, and lacking in our experience.

The key to changing this mindset is to shift our attention. When we think outside the box, we begin to realize that the box, our perceived boundaries, and any limitations are not real. Nothing holds us back from the solutions we want to obtain, the endless creative possibilities we wish to experience, and the life we desire. Thinking outside the box means adopting the mindset and belief that all things are possible—even the things we have never thought of or considered before.

This is the very nature of living from a high consciousness divine perspective. Maybe this kind of thinking seems unusual, confusing, and hard. It is true that your human ego may not fully understand, but your higher self fully understands and knows the value of unrestricted, "outside the box" thinking.

Affirm

When my thoughts are unlimited,
my life experience becomes unlimited.

SOMETIMES IT'S NOT THE THING
SEPTEMBER 7

A client once came to me wishing to experience more peace in her life. She was troubled by the things her husband wrote about on the internet. He frequently embellished his version of stories, and she disagreed with much of what he wrote to his thousands of followers. She carried around with her such resentment, anger, and frustration. We talked about how she could honor her feelings and still live in alignment with her spiritual Truth.

She blurted out, "I feel fine except when I read his blogs." I pretended I didn't hear her and asked her to repeat herself. "I'm fine as long as I don't read his blogs!" she said again.

"You mean you feel peaceful?" I prodded.

"Yes!" Realization struck, and she laughed. "Oh my God, I need to stop reading them!" It wasn't about her husband at all. She needed to stop doing the activity that took away her peace. Sometimes, it is as simple as recognizing that we are the ones stopping ourselves from experiencing peace. She was choosing to do an activity that robbed her of her peace.

The next time you feel discomfort, irritation, chaos—stop and consider the choice you are making.

Ask

Is it about the thing,
or is it about my choice to do the thing?

THE OPPORTUNITIES ARE THERE
SEPTEMBER 8

Imagine you live in a city with great resources available to you, things like access to nature, music, art, literature, entertainment, education, etc. You have endless opportunities to gain knowledge and appreciation of all aspects of life! It is all free for the taking and enjoying. Now, picture millions of people living in this city with you, completely unaware of these privileges. Perhaps some of the people are aware, but they don't care. They go on about their day, living in ignorance, completely ignoring what is available to them.

This is what spiritual awareness is like. It is always there—whatever method, practice, ritual, or teaching we wish to use to explore it. If one method doesn't work, we are free to find another. Whatever God, Spirit, Universe, Source we seek is always there, waiting for our attention and awareness. We can choose to engage, participate, learn, study, and grow in our divine spiritual Truth, or we can pass it by and live in human ignorance. This is not said with judgment of any sort, but to remind us the choice is always ours to make.

Affirm

*Today, I choose to shift my awareness
to the Divine in whatever way I see fit.*

WHAT'S WORKING RIGHT?
SEPTEMBER 9

In this very moment, can you identify which body systems or organs in your body are working at their optimum level? We don't think about that very often. So much must be functioning and working well in your body to sustain your life. Think about this: Most of us at some point have experienced a splitting headache—pain radiating in our temples, our forehead, and all around our eyes. You can't think about anything else but that headache. But how often, when we are not experiencing a headache, do we stop and say, "Gee, my head is feeling great today. The muscles around my head are relaxed and working well."

Shift your attention and think about how much in your body is not only functioning, but operating at the optimal, prime level of intelligence. Your heart is beating at a perfect rhythm, pumping blood to every organ in your body. Your lungs are taking in and expelling oxygen at the perfect levels, transferring it to your bloodstream. Your stomach is digesting your food, breaking it down to give you energy. There is so much in our body that deserves our attention, focus, and gratitude!

Affirm

I give thanks for all the organs, systems, and trillions of cells in my body that are functioning in Divine Intelligence right now.

MANIFESTATION VS. RESTORATION
SEPTEMBER 10

Your natural state of being is spiritually perfect, whole, and complete. If we truly believe this, that each one of us exists as an expression of the Divine, then what, if anything, needs to be healed in us? Belief in our unity with God is key. Can God lack health, love, joy, peace, etc.? Of course not. God is all these things. If we are not experiencing them, we look to our thought. We look to our understanding of our unity with God. We look to our belief in the availability and presence of our good. It is always there.

When we experience these good things, did we manifest them? Create them? Did we create our health, wealth, peace, and joy? Or did we simply allow the Divine within us to instinctively express in, through, and as us, revealing our natural state of being? Perhaps it isn't a manifestation as much as it is a restoration of our true nature. A revealing of our Divine Truth.

Affirm

Everything that God is, I am.
My natural state of spiritual perfection is revealed.

WHY SPIRITUALITY MATTERS
SEPTEMBER 11

Deep spiritual thinkers understand the unity of all life. We know and trust in our own divinity, and we try to see that divinity in others. We hold space for the devastated, and we choose to be the presence of love and light in the world. We do the study, the spiritual practice, and the work to be higher-consciousness people, which makes us a powerful force in the world.

This matters because the world seems to be experiencing increasingly violent, chaotic, divisive, life-changing events—events that have the potential to change the trajectory of humanity, of life on earth. Whatever human devastation we might experience, there is always "the other side" of it afterward.

Wars end. Elections happen. Fires burn out. Storm recovery takes place. The sun comes out again. On the other side, the highly conscious, spiritually aware people might be the reason life continues in a new, more unified way.

Affirm

I matter. My beliefs matter. My spirituality matters.

IT ALWAYS SAYS YES!
SEPTEMBER 12

Before I learned about New Thought principles, I did not understand the importance of being mindful of my speech and what I declared about my life. I didn't know that the Universe always says "YES" to what we say. I thought I was being funny back then when I would complain about my problems and say things like, "Ugh, I hate my life!"

The Universe, the Spirit within me, was always listening and saying yes. "You hate your life? Let's create more of that together—more things to hate!" I experienced chaos, destruction, and problems. Things broke down all around me. I had car repairs, unexpected bills, plumbing leaks, mold in my house, and even a neighbor's tree fell on my roof! I was creating chaos for myself and my family.

Now I know the value of being mindful of my speech. We cannot underestimate our ability to transform our lives by the renewing of our minds and by affirming good things about our lives and the lives of others. If you find yourself accidentally complaining, speaking negatively to yourself or others, you can gently, lovingly make the choice in that moment to speak differently. Spirit within you is always listening, ready to say yes to your thoughts and words.

Affirm

I am mindful of my speech because Spirit always says,
"Yes" to what I think, affirm, and say.

A PRAYER FOR THE COLLECTIVE
SEPTEMBER 13

Pray

The One Power of God is all there is, and It is expressed in all life. This Divine Power for good is at the center of all people, always. I live and move and have my being in this One Power. I know this is true for me, and I know it is true for everyone. In this moment, I choose to recognize the beautiful power of community. I choose to see beyond made-up human labels and divisions to the deep sense of belonging that comes from just being a child of the Divine. I choose to be led by Spirit, to work in ways that co-create with my brothers and sisters. I know when we do this together, we can expect a reality that is a harmonious, empowering, collective experience.

This is what I say yes to. This is what we affirm together. I give great thanks for the opportunity that is before us in this moment, and in the next moment, and in every moment that we choose to live in this state of consciousness. I am so grateful that this is the way life works, and that this is the way we are empowered together. I let this prayer go, fully anticipating its fulfillment.

And So It Is. Amen.

MEDITATION TIPS
SEPTEMBER 14

Meditation is an incredible spiritual practice that millions of people use daily. Are you one of the countless people who have tried meditation and felt like they failed at it? Consider the following five tips as encouragement to try meditation again.

Act

• *Try short periods of time. Just five minutes of meditation each day counts! Gradually increase the amount of time you sit in the stillness each day.*

• *Keep at it daily. They call it spiritual practice for a reason, so keep practicing. Set the goal to do it daily for an entire month and see how you do. Let it become a habit.*

• *Eliminate distractions. Can you find a time when you will not be disturbed by anyone? Can you turn off your phone and commit to the practice with no interruptions, fully connecting with Spirit?*

• *Try nature. Have you considered that a walk in nature by yourself can be a form of meditation? Focus on the colors you see, the sounds you hear—the wind, the birds, the trees swaying, etc. Nature is a wonderful way to connect with Life.*

• *Pay attention to your breath. Long, deep breaths help us focus on the present moment. Can you recognize that you are being breathed by Spirit? Use your breath to ground yourself and allow yourself to fully relax in the moment.*

MAKE THE MEAL HAPPY!
SEPTEMBER 15

Everyone has heard of a certain "Happy Meal™" sold for children at a particular fast food restaurant. These meals are designed and marketed to bring joy to kids, complete with colorful, entertaining packaging and a toy. Why is joy something only marketed to children's meals and not adults? Why aren't adults joyful when we eat?

The answer might lie in where our minds are focused while eating. Are we in a rush? Are we enjoying the company of those around us while we eat? Is there pleasant conversation and laughter? Do we even like the food we are eating? Are we feeling grateful that our food is nourishing our bodies? Is what we're eating promoting our health or potentially contributing to our lack of health?

Think about these things the next time you sit down to eat. Use it as a chance to infuse your digestive system with joy. Having a meal can be an opportunity to experience happiness.

Affirm

Today, I am mindful of the happiness I experience while eating.

BE THE GOOD
SEPTEMBER 16

The idea of "evil" has nothing to do with any perceived entity outside us, intending to hurt us. A better way to look at evil is to view it as the manifestation of our own negative thoughts and imagination. In other words, the more we believe in evil, the more "evil" we will see—the more negative, difficult, unwanted things we will experience. The question then becomes: Why would you ever want to have a negative thought if it could potentially bring a negative experience upon you?

What if we counteracted every negative thought with multiple positive thoughts of good unfolding in humanity? Can you think of examples of good in the world? There are so many. Once you start looking for them, the more you will notice. When you notice them, dwell on them!

I once ate in a restaurant that had a large sign that read: FREE FOOD if you present a declined debit card caused by lack of funds. Another time in a restaurant I watched one table pay for another table's bill because they overheard them discussing a serious diagnosis. I once opened my front door to discover boxes of groceries my friends had dropped off because I had to miss a week of work to take care of my daughter after she broke her arm and needed surgery. Good is always happening in the world. If you struggle to find examples of good unfolding in your life, perhaps it is your opportunity to be the good.

Act

BE-lieve in THE GOOD.

A NEW WAY TO WORRY
SEPTEMBER 17

A famous quote frequently attributed to American humorist Erma Bombeck says, "Worry is like a rocking chair; it gives you something to do but never gets you anywhere." Worry is more than that—it is actually a misuse of Spiritual Law. We know what we are focused on with our imagination creates our reality. Do not use your energy to worry. Instead, use your energy to believe in the outcome you wish you see, to imagine the experience you want to have, and to envision the possibility of your good being revealed to you.

Your energy, thoughts, and intentions are so powerful. Use them to believe in what you desire. Something to consider: What if you worried about the best-case scenario and best-possible outcome to whatever has you concerned? Most people forget this is always an option! We can use our time, thought, energy, and imagination to "worry" about our best possible life, our highest possible good. Give it a try. Test it to see if it creates better life experiences for you!

Affirm

Today, I intend to think about my best-case scenario.

NOTHING TO FEAR
SEPTEMBER 18

Fear is believing there is something that God doesn't know, God can't handle, or God can't understand. This is simply not possible. Who do we think we are to not only be afraid, but express that fear, talk about it, and argue for it? When we are thinking, believing, and living from a place of fear, we are believing in our separateness from the Divine.

You are not separate from the Divine. You do not have to fear any human condition, circumstance, or situation. Take a moment to breathe. Remember the Truth of who and what you are. Stand firm in your faith.

There is nothing God can't handle. God not only knows all but is present in all your human experiences. You are fully surrounded, supported, and loved. There is nothing to fear.

Affirm

I am loved. There is nothing to fear. All is well.

ALL YOU NEED
SEPTEMBER 19

A famous quote by actor Charlie Chaplin says: "You need power only when you want to do something harmful; otherwise, love is enough to get everything done." Love is the most powerful force in the universe. Where can you use love as your power to accomplish something? For instance,

Can loving what you do get you the job you want?
Can loving your spouse make your relationship more harmonious?
Can loving yourself improve your health?
Can loving what you already have increase your prosperity?

You are extraordinarily powerful because of the love within you. Act from a place of love. Move from a place of love. Respond from a place of love. Think from a place of love.

Affirm

The love within me is powerful.
It is always enough to get everything done.

ONE SOURCE
SEPTEMBER 20

Everyone has experienced lack at some point in life, whether it is from an unexpected bill, a change in job status, a pay cut, or simply poor budgeting. We need money for food, shelter, and other basic human needs. The resources need to come from somewhere.

The truth is, there is only One Source of all resources, and that inexhaustible supply expresses to and through each of us, individually. The next time it seems like you don't have enough money, trust in your unity and oneness with the Source of all abundance. Trust that your needs are met and your unlimited good is available to you. The supply of life is endless and can appear in any number of unexpected and surprising ways.

Affirm

I am one with the Source of all; all my needs are met.

LOOK FOR IT
SEPTEMBER 21

I have a rock garden in front of my house filled with hundreds of heart-shaped rocks. A friend of mine came to visit and noticed them as she came to the door. Impressed, she asked me how I found all those heart-shaped rocks. I told her, "I look for them!"

It sounds stupid, but yes, the way I find heart rocks is to look for them. This is how we find anything we desire, and this is a key to life. We find what we look for. I am fortunate to live by the ocean, and I walk on the beach almost every day. When I am walking on the beach, I am always looking for a heart rock, scanning the sand as I go, looking for exactly what I want to find. I find so many because I am actively looking for them.

This applies to anything in life. If you're looking for trouble, you're going to find trouble. If you're looking for anger and hate, you're going to find anger and hate. If you're looking for your good that you want to experience, or something specific you desire, you're going to find it. You just have to be focused on it, actively looking for it, and fully expecting to find it constantly. It is the Law of Attraction. You find what you're looking for. So, the question is, what are you looking for?

Affirm

Today, I am committed to look for my good,
fully expecting for it to be revealed to me.

HOW TO WIN EVERY CONTEST
SEPTEMBER 22

Imagine a big sports game is taking place, and you are very invested in a particular outcome. Maybe you even placed a bet on a particular team—your favorite team, or maybe an election is happening, and you worked hard and campaigned for a certain candidate. If your team or candidate loses, you feel like you lost, too. You were emotionally invested and now feel sad. But what if there were a way to ensure you won every sporting event, every contest, every election?

You are the real winner if, no matter what happens, no matter who is declared the winner, you maintain your sense of peace, harmony, and love. No outcome of any contest, election, or test, can take these things from you. Keep your awareness centered in this Truth. When you can protect your mental health and know that no matter what takes place, you are still you, you can still show up in this world as Spirit. You're the real winner if you know beyond a shadow of a doubt that you are still whole and complete in the Divine. No outer experience can change the Divine Truth of who and what you are.

Affirm

I am the real winner of all contests.
Nothing can separate me from my Divine Truth.

THIS IS A FRIENDLY UNIVERSE
SEPTEMBER 23

Albert Einstein told us that, "The most important decision we have to make is whether we believe in a friendly or hostile universe." What a challenge it is to choose friendliness, love, compassion, and unity, when hostility and hatred are so prevalent. We can faithfully make this choice, to move forward in hope, believing in a loving, friendly universe, even when the evidence shows us otherwise. Consciously making this decision is an important part of our spiritual practice.

Believing in a friendly universe does not mean denying pain, conflict, or injustice. It means trusting that, beneath the appearances, capital L-Life is moving toward healing, wholeness, and the greater good. Our true power is not found in controlling outer circumstances, but in our capacity to meet them with a loving, conscious state of being.

This power is always available to you. Where can you apply it? The next time you encounter troubling news, a personal conflict, or someone expressing hostility, consider it an invitation to meet the moment with love rather than fear. Life is always giving us the opportunity to decide how we will interpret and engage with our experience. We choose the story we live in. What story are you choosing to tell yourself?

Affirm

I choose to view my life as a friendly, loving, compassionate expression of the Divine—even when it appears otherwise— especially when it appears otherwise!
I believe there is always a positive lesson unfolding in my experience.

ARE YOU A LIGHTWORKER?
SEPTEMBER 24

A lightworker is a person who consciously decides to devote their life to bringing positive energy and healing to the world through love, compassion, and empathy. They often feel a higher calling to help others and believe in their potential to create positive change. Your energy, your high vibration, makes the world a brighter place. Never forget this, no matter what dark situation you may find yourself participating in or witnessing.

Lightworkers do not always live in positivity, love, and light. On the contrary, being a lightworker involves confronting your own shadow and doing the inner work necessary to live in alignment with Source as much as possible. You don't have to be "fully enlightened" or "illumined" to be considered a lightworker. I believe we are all lightworkers at various moments in our lives. It is our commitment to our conscious effort that is key.

The world needs the light workers.
You are the light. Keep shining.

Affirm

I am the opportunity to show up as Divine Love in this world.
I am the Light!

THAT'S DEEP
SEPTEMBER 25

Have you ever spent time in a boat on the ocean? You quickly learn that on the surface, you might find choppy waters that can be chaotic and turbulent, uncomfortable and scary. But if you have the proper equipment to dive deeper, you will find that the same waters are actually calm and still. This is a spiritual lesson!

If we take the time to go there mentally, to the deep recesses of our mind, in the stillness of our body, we remember and realize our Truth. Let the stillness feed your spirit and remind you of who and what you are. Life is about balance, calm, and peace. In the tranquil stillness of your mind, you are the perfect expression of Divine Life.

Affirm

At the center of my being, all is well.
I am calm, centered, and peaceful.

STOP DOING THIS...
SEPTEMBER 26

Much of this book encourages you to do something, like shifting your perspective, exploring a particular spiritual practice, or considering a new way to think. This entry encourages you to *stop* doing two things that are detrimental to our well-being.

1. Stop imagining bad things.
Humans are constantly imagining bad things that could happen. Of the potential 60,000 thoughts we think per day, 80% of them are negative. Choose in this moment to stop using your imagination for negative outcomes.

2. Stop reacting as if the bad things you imagine have already happened.
Your imagination, your thoughts, and your energy are very powerful. When we imagine bad things, it sets the Creative Process in motion. We make it worse when we pick up the ball and run with the imagined negative thought, reacting in our bodies as if the thing has already happened, feeling the tension, and sensing the stress. Can you catch yourself and imagine the opposite? Can you imagine peace, serenity, harmony, and love instead?

Ask

How would I feel if I stopped reacting to imagined fears?

Affirm

*Today, I commit to stop imagining bad things,
and I choose to stop reacting as if those bad things have already happened.*

INSTABILITY AND AWAKENING
SEPTEMBER 27

What if negative situations happening in the world are actually causing humanity to spiritually awaken faster? Could pain and suffering lead to more conscious realization? Consider how outraged and angry people were during the late 1960s and early 1970s. The tumultuous era included the Civil Rights Movement, the Vietnam War, activism, protests, violence, a renewed focus on social justice, etc. As difficult as that time in history was to endure, we can see it created positive outcomes and brought about beneficial shifts in humanity.

Instability brings about human change. Through it all, there is the constant Truth of God—the realization of our oneness. Globally and nationally, we can always look at destructive times as an awakening that is taking place. Times like these create shifts in consciousness. Take heart. Do your inner work, love one another, and remember the Truth.

Affirm

*I know when I see world devastation and national turmoil,
it is bringing about a spiritual awakening.
I am part of it; I know the Truth of our oneness.*

FOUR LITTLE PHRASES... BIG RESULTS
SEPTEMBER 28

Ho'oponopono, the ancient Hawaiian practice of reconciliation and forgiveness, involves speaking, thinking, or writing the following four statements:

I love you.
I'm sorry.
Please forgive me.
Thank you.

The "I love you" statement can be said first or last. There are numerous ways the practice can be done, with the ultimate goal being to transform relationships, shift your feelings about a situation, promote self-healing, facilitate forgiveness, and create balance. The statements can be focused on during meditation, used as journal prompts, or simply chanted as a mantra.

This practice can be used for any situation for which you seek healing. For example, if you were diagnosed with an illness, you could write the statements to your body, telling it how much you love it and promise to take better care of it. You could acknowledge that you are sorry for ways you have mistreated or neglected your body. You could ask it for forgiveness, releasing the past and freeing yourself from the situation. You could thank your body for all the ways it keeps you alive, healthy, and in balance.

Ask

*Where in my life can I creatively use
the powerful spiritual practice of ho'oponopono?*

REMEMBER TO CIRCLE BACK
SEPTEMBER 29

Have you ever been filled with rage over a decision that was out of your control? For instance, when management makes a decision about the way things are handled at your work, or when a new law is passed by the government that you wholeheartedly disagree with? We are allowed to feel outrage when things like this happen, but at what point does it harm us to do so?

Even though feeling rage is part of being human, it does not serve your well-being. In fact, it harms you. The goal is to not be in a state of rage all the time. It takes conscious effort to stay in balance—to acknowledge feelings of frustration, then to take the time to circle back to the Truth, letting peace return. This is part of being human.

Where are you today on the spectrum? If you are angry or outraged, give yourself some grace. Can you release the feelings and come back to center?

When I feel enraged over a particular situation, I use the emotion as a reminder that I cannot serve others if I am forgetting to take care of my own mental health first.

Affirm

I deserve peace.
I let the anger go and circle back to the Truth.

THAT'S BEAUTIFUL!
SEPTEMBER 30

Appreciate the beauty all around you. Make this your challenge today. Look around your life, your home, your community, your world, and make a list of all that is beautiful. You've heard the saying, *beauty is in the eye of the beholder*, and that's the best part of this challenge. You are to acknowledge the things *you* find beautiful.

Beauty brings us joy and lifts our spirits when we see it. How often do we make a point to seek it out and recognize it? Do this challenge with someone else; then compare your lists. Perhaps they see something beautiful you missed.

Affirm

*Today, my intention is to see and appreciate the beauty all around me.
I allow it to lift my spirit and bring me joy.*

OCTOBER

THE STORY
OCTOBER 1

We all have a human story about our identity—what we call ourselves and go by, what we do for a living, who we are in relation to others, our gender, ethnicity, cultural background, class, education, personality traits, etc. This story is ego-based and often very superficial. Our human story tells us that we are separate from each other, that where my awareness ends, yours begins, that we can and often do operate against one another.

We know that spiritually, none of this is true. We are all one, expressing from the same Source. I express in you, and you express in me. We are designed to love and support each other in unity and harmony.

Ask

*What happens when I let go of my human story—
even just for a moment of contemplative meditation?
Who am I without my story?
Who is my neighbor without their story?*

Affirm

I am not my human story.

THOUGHTS: GO DEEPER
OCTOBER 2

It can be exhausting to pay attention to your thoughts. All we can do is make our best effort to remind ourselves to notice them. But, then what? We weed out the negative ones. When you realize you are thinking a thought that does not feel good, that doesn't feel true to you, how do you fix it?

One way to fix the thought and really change it is to ask yourself: Why do I believe that? We have lots of thoughts floating around in our heads all the time. Usually, we don't even stop to think about them. But when you take a moment to pause and say, "Okay, this is what I'm thinking," and then go further to the question—But why do I believe that? *This* is how we fix our thinking. Use these questions to get to the root of what is really going on with your thoughts.

Ask

Why do I believe that?
Was I taught that in my childhood?
Do I have family members that also believe that?
Is this something society has told me to believe?
Is this thought an opinion I saw in the media?
Is this thought really true?
Could I think something different?

Affirm

I am free to notice and question my thoughts
so I can live in alignment with my true divine self.

GOD IS...I AM
OCTOBER 3

Affirm

If God is Love, I am Love.
If God is Peace, I am Peace.
If God is Joy, I am Joy.
If God is Abundance, I am Abundance.
If God is Prosperity, I am Prosperity.
If God is Health, I am Health.
If God is Wholeness, I am Wholeness.
If God is Balance, I am Balance.
If God is Creativity, I am Creativity.
If God is Intelligence, I am Intelligence.
If God is Wisdom, I am Wisdom.
If God is… I Am.

TIS THE SEASON
OCTOBER 4

If you were asked to name a *season* or describe what that word means, your mind may immediately go to the four divisions of the calendar year that are marked by weather patterns and daylight: spring, summer, fall, and winter. Maybe you are into sports, and you would talk to me about football season or baseball season, or whatever your favorite athletic pastime is. Perhaps your mind goes to your favorite holiday season. Who knows? Maybe you pay close attention to a certain season of produce. I, for one, really enjoy fresh pomegranate season!

I doubt a single person would talk about cold and flu season. Cold and flu season isn't real. It is not a naturally occurring part of human life. It is a made-up construct to get you focused on catching a cold and getting the flu, putting the thought of sickness into your conscious awareness. If you notice, much of the marketing done by drug and cold medicine manufacturers reference this "season" to get you to stock up on their product and be prepared when you are "inevitably" struck ill.

The truth is, we don't have to listen to and participate in this mindset anymore because we know better.

Affirm

A particular time of year poses no threat to my well-being.
I am healthy, whole, and complete all year long.

SHH... WE'RE SHOPPING HERE
OCTOBER 5

Once while shopping in a grocery store, a stranger began ranting to me about the price of groceries, his political stance on certain policy issues, and how his support of a particular political candidate would somehow help. I had not asked for his opinion on these matters. He just began aggressively sharing, unprovoked. Everything shifted in the moment as my discomfort spread and I felt my body tense. In that moment, I wanted him to stop talking and be quiet. But he didn't. He continued talking. As politely as possible, I removed myself from the situation and said goodbye.

My desire for him to be quiet felt like a spiritual lesson. In the quiet, in the silence, in the stillness, is often where it is easier to see the divinity in our fellow man. If I had argued with him, shared the opposite side of America's political policy choices, ranted about my thoughts about economics, etc., it would not have served either of us. It would not have brought us together, nor would it have helped him see our unity and oneness. There is a time and a place for debate, discussion, and deliberation. There is also a time to be quiet, silent, and still.

Affirm

I intuitively know when it is time to be quiet and still.
I know the oneness of humanity.

VISUALIZATION WORKS
OCTOBER 6

Psychologists have proven that the human nervous system cannot differentiate between an actual experience and an experience that is imagined. That is why when you close your eyes and imagine that you are biting into a juicy red apple, your mouth salivates. Your mouth waters simply because you went there in your mind. You used your senses. You thought about how the apple looks, how it smells, whether it is firm or soft, the sound of the crunch, and the taste of that sweet, juicy bite in your mouth.

The process of visualization is based on the power and energy of the Universe. There is a connection between the power of our mind and outpicturing of our imagined, visualized thought. We can use the spiritual practice of visualization for anything. Athletes run their event or play the sport in their minds and the muscles fire in their body in the same sequence as when they are performing in reality. It is like extra practice to improve their skills!

FYI, you are holding a published book in your hands that was long ago just visualized in the mind of the author. Visualization works! There is no limit to how we can apply this spiritual strategy.

Ask

What can I use visualization to create, experience, or become?

IT COULD GO RIGHT
OCTOBER 7

Whenever I worried as a young girl, complaining and expecting the worst thing to happen, my father would stop me and ask, "But what could go right?" He was certainly never aware of New Thought spiritual principle; that wasn't his religion or the spiritual tradition he practiced. It was just how he chose to parent me, to try to get me to shift my thinking to expect a positive outcome. It took many years for me to catch on and take his message to heart, but I finally did. As an adult, his influence made a huge difference in my life.

Encouraging young people to accentuate the positive, stay focused on the outcomes they wish to see, and live in alignment with the Truth of their divine nature are powerful ways to ultimately influence the collective consciousness. As younger generations are exposed to and learn these New Thought principles, the sooner we will see a world that works for everyone. Next time you hear a young person complaining and expecting a bad outcome, ask them, "But what could go right?"

Affirm

*When I find myself lost in negative thoughts,
I remember to stop and ask myself, "What could go right?"*

A PROSPERITY/ABUNDANCE TEST
OCTOBER 8

If you focus on what you lack, you experience more lack. If you focus on what you have, and you have gratitude for it, you receive more. More abundance, more prosperity, more love, more everything. What we focus on expands and grows. This is Spiritual Law. We don't need to complain about what we don't have or what we need or what we want. Instead, we can look around at the good that we are already experiencing in our lives and celebrate it. We can have gratitude and be happy about it. It is Spiritual Law that it will expand and grow.

Skeptical? Good for you—only highly intelligent people are skeptical! Test this philosophy for yourself and see. Spend time each day thinking, writing, and talking about all the good you have in your life, whether material things or nonmaterial things. See if your attention and gratitude make them grow. What do you have to lose?

Affirm

*I choose to focus my attention and
gratitude on all the good in my life.*

PERCEPTIONS CAN BE WRONG
OCTOBER 9

A famous Taoist parable describes a man who was rowing his rowboat upstream on a misty morning. The man sees another boat coming downstream, right toward him. He shouts for them to be careful, but the boat hits his and it nearly sinks. He is full of anger, yelling at the other person before he realizes there is no person in the other boat. It had just gotten loose and happened to come downstream. His anger vanished, and he felt silly and laughed.

How often are our perceptions wrong? We allow ourselves to be full of bad feelings that negatively impact our experience. Can you look deeper to understand the true nature of what is happening? Your response to and your feelings about events are within your control. They are always a decision!

How often are we responding to an empty boat, a big nothing that just happens to be in our way? The Buddha taught that we must be one with what we want to understand. When we recognize that we are one with everything—everything we love and everything we hate, everything that we think could possibly stand in our way—we realize that all of it is actually nothing. The way of understanding is to let go of our knowledge in order to transcend whatever is before us that we perceive as a block to our future. This is divine intervention. This is the moment we allow the Divine to penetrate our heart—our life.

Affirm

I can always look beyond my perceptions and feelings.
I am open to divine intervention.

SOLUTIONS EXIST
OCTOBER 10

Every problem has a solution. So often human beings wring our hands with worry, complaint, whining, and struggle, when we can instead choose to affirm, believe, and trust that every problem has a solution. Spirit doesn't know anything about problems; it only knows solutions. When we get our consciousness to the belief in that possibility—to that way of thinking and believing that there is a solution to absolutely any problem we could experience—*that's* how problems get solved. *That* is when the answers are revealed, once we believe that a solution not only exists, but that it can be revealed to us.

Affirm

There is a solution to every problem.
I can access all the divine solutions available to me.

SOME REALLY GOOD CHEESE
OCTOBER 11

Having gratitude is a powerful spiritual practice that helps draw more good to us. Being thankful for even little things in our lives keeps us in a state of appreciation and in the flow of abundance. Once you start using this practice regularly, you see how much it impacts your life.

I was once on the phone with my daughter and happened to mention to her that I got some really good cheese. She was confused.

"Wait, what did you just say?" she asked.

"I got some really great cheese!" I told her excitedly. I was very serious.

She laughed at me and couldn't believe I said something so silly. But it was true! My day was lifted because I so enjoyed some delicious cheese I had bought. I was grateful and wanted to tell her about it!

Normalize talking about the things you are grateful for and appreciate, no matter how silly, how small, or how strange.

Ask

What did I love and appreciate about my day?

DON'T BE A MONKEY
OCTOBER 12

There are over 600 different species of monkeys. Most live in the African jungles. When a zoo in America needs monkeys, zoologists have to catch them in Africa. They don't want to hurt or traumatize the monkeys. So, they take big, heavy, skinny-necked ceramic bottles with them. They drop some sweet-smelling nuts in the bottles and place them on the floor of the jungle. Then they wait.

They come back the next day, and inevitably, there is a monkey trapped next to every bottle, just sitting there. The monkey comes along, and it smells the nuts in the bottle. It investigates the bottle, putting its arm inside to get the nuts. The monkey closes its hand around the nuts, and then it is trapped. It can't get its hand out of the bottle because it won't let go of the nuts. The bottle is too heavy to lift, so it is trapped.

This sounds ridiculous, but in many ways, we are like the trapped monkeys. We often keep a tight grip on our circumstances, our perceived problems, our thoughts of lack, and our false beliefs. We don't want to let go of them and be free. The monkey has a closed fist that traps it next to the bottle, but it's not really trapped. It is its own doing. Sometimes we are trapped because we close our minds to the possibility of miracles in our life. We close our minds to believing these principles with all our being. *That's* what we need to open our minds to—our spiritual Truth. We have to not only let go of but also see beyond the conditions before us.

Affirm

I am not trapped.
I am open to the possibility of miracles in my life.

REPEAT AFTER ME
OCTOBER 13

Looking for a way to instantly lift your consciousness? Take several deep breaths, be still, and close your eyes as you repeat the following mantra ten, fifty, or 100 times. Do it until you feel a shift in consciousness.

Affirm

The only thing that matters is my awareness of God.
The only thing that matters is my awareness of God.
The only thing that matters is my awareness of God.
The only thing that matters is my awareness of God.
The only thing that matters is my awareness of God.
The only thing that matters is my awareness of God.
The only thing that matters is my awareness of God.
The only thing that matters is my awareness of God.
The only thing that matters is my awareness of God.
The only thing that matters is my awareness of God.

WHEN THEY ARE HARD TO LOVE
OCTOBER 14

Stop and think for a moment about the people in your life whom you may have difficulty loving. Call them to mind. Perhaps take a moment to write them down. Hopefully, there aren't many.

Identify the traits in these individuals that you find difficult to love. What do you think it is that specifically causes the difficulty? What behaviors and traits do they exhibit that cause these problems? What gets under your skin about them? List these traits.

Ask

Are any of these traits in me? Where do I see these traits unfolding in my own behaviors, actions, and demeanor? If I notice the traits, can I give myself grace, compassion, and love? Can I offer the same to the individuals with whom I am having difficulty?

Take this exercise even deeper: What is the Christlike/divine quality I can practice with these people in my life that could help the relationship? List these divine qualities and meditate on them. Are these divine traits present in this moment? (How could they not be, when the Divine is always present?)

When I look deeply, do I see these divine qualities in my loved ones? Do I see them in myself?

Affirm

*I am willing to go within to heal my relationships
so I can live my best life in harmony, oneness, and love.*

ALL DAY LONG
OCTOBER 15

The goal of our human experience (and mind you, it is a lofty goal) is to unify in consciousness with Spirit as much as possible, to shift our awareness to the God-Presence within. We do this "shifting" via spiritual practice, through prayer, meditation, and by constantly resetting our mental attitude and thought.

A minister once acknowledged in a sermon, "I think about God all day long." I had never heard someone say such a thing! The comment sounded over the top and obsessive, but it is this sort of admission that helps us understand the kind of mental work necessary to be in a state of higher consciousness. For some of us, though, this doesn't come naturally. It feels like hard work! We forget we can bring this concern to Spirit and ask for help.

When we ask the Universe to show us all the ways we can get to and maintain this state of awareness, it delivers. Working with spiritual principles doesn't have to be confusing, overwhelming, or hard. Start by believing that a higher consciousness can come easily to you. Why can't it? Ask for and believe you will see examples of divine characteristics in your daily life, and you will see them. Expect Divine Truth to consume your human experience, and it will.

Affirm

*All day, every day, I am willing to do
the necessary spiritual work to align with Spirit.*

A PRAYER FOR YOU
OCTOBER 16

Pray

Today, I stand in the Truth that all things are possible. I am confident in the love found deep within each person. All humanity is united in the Truth of their divinity. I go within to the Peace, Love, and Joy of God. There is peace in this moment. There is love in this moment. There is joy in this moment. My awareness of these Truths is what makes them so.

I know who I am and where I belong, and it is with God as a divine soul, an expression of the One, the One that is All, the One that is here now in this moment as me. I am here as God's Peace. I am here as God's Love. I am here as God's Joy. I am the opportunity to show up as Spirit. I am so thankful to be this and to do this, but most of all, I am thankful for the ability to understand this. Thoughts like this lift my consciousness, and that, in turn, lifts the collective consciousness. I understand my divine nature and the divine nature of the world. All is well. I am loved, and I am here to love.

And So It Is. Amen.

SPIRITUAL HEALTH MATTERS
OCTOBER 17

Your ego does not want you to remember that you are a divine, eternal soul. The more you practice spirituality and remind yourself of this (whether through meditating, sitting in the stillness, praying, reading inspirational books like this one, or some other spiritual practice), the more peaceful and balanced your life experience will be.

You wouldn't ignore your body's health. You would notice and pay attention to symptoms of illness, disease, or pain. You would likely do something to alleviate the situation, like go see a doctor or take a pain reliever. You wouldn't ignore your mental health either —at least I hope you wouldn't! You would seek professional help, like a counselor, therapist, or psychologist.

So, why would you ignore your soul's health by not tending to your spiritual needs? It is good for your soul to cultivate your spiritual Truth. This is how we receive guidance, inspiration, and solutions.

Affirm

Today, and every day, I choose to cultivate my spiritual Truth.
My eternal soul appreciates my attention.

RELAX
OCTOBER 18

Often we are told we should "seek God" and "seek God's kingdom," but what if that's not actually true? Perhaps we don't need to seek. What if we really just need to rest in the stillness and silence, focused on the Truth of our eternal life in God being revealed to us? To seek is work. Seek is a verb, an action word. It means to go in search of, to go to, or to try to find. This would imply God is somewhere else other than right where we are. To seek sounds frantic and confusing—we seek things that we have lost and things we struggle without.

Knowing and receiving Divine Truth is not frantic. It is calm, peaceful, reassuring, and can happen over time. God does not and cannot withhold any good thing we could possibly ask for, such as peace, love, joy, abundance, health, wisdom, power, freedom, etc. It is up to us to be still and willingly receive. We cannot actively seek to bring God to us when God is already here. It is up to us to be in a state of open, unlimited receptivity in our awareness.

Remember, you cannot frantically grip and hold on to something that is always already within you. Relax. It is safe to let your humanness fall away. Become comfortable with the infiniteness of God and your unity with It. What is left but God?

Affirm

*Today, I remember that nothing matters but my awareness of God.
I and my Father are One. (John 10:30)*

ONE YEAR FROM NOW
OCTOBER 19

Imagine your life one year from now. From that moment in the future, imagine you are looking backward, remembering what is happening in your life right now. "Now" is your past in this scenario. You're seeing the problems and troubles of today, but they're in the past. You notice something very interesting. In this future moment, a year from now, you are grateful. You are grateful for those troubles you had.

It turns out from this one year in the future perspective, the thing that troubled you so much, kept you up at night, and made you feel so distraught and powerless is actually the thing you are most grateful for. Imagine that! It's ironic and almost funny. You feel jubilant, relieved, and happy. What a blessing that little problem was! Look how it all turned out in just a year!

Though this exercise may seem weird, this is how we dissolve our troubles and shape them into the life we desire. Visualization and gratitude are spiritual practices that complement each other well. You can powerfully transform your life by visualizing the outcome you wish to see and having gratitude for even your biggest problems.

Affirm

*I am grateful for every seeming problem I experience
because troubles are always opportunities for positive transitions.*

MORE THAN THIS WORLD
OCTOBER 20

When the world gets you down, it helps to remember that this isn't the only world. There is a lot more to life than just this human experience. You are a soul, and life is eternal. Nothing can hurt your life or take your life. There is more than this world that we are living in. This is not only a comforting thought, but it is also the truth.

Being human is an experience that we don't have to take so seriously. Remember, being in a human body is an experience that your soul chose. I would even venture to say that your soul was excited to sign up for this experience! It wanted to be here right now, at this time in history, with your exact family, with your childhood, in your body, experiencing these lessons. They call it "Earth School" for a reason.

Ask

Why did my soul choose this particular expression
for me at this time in history?
Are thoughts like this overwhelming or empowering?

THE POWER OF YOUR IMAGINATION
OCTOBER 21

We hear that all things are possible, and we want to believe it, but is this spiritual idea really true? Can I take off and fly around the room or manifest a million dollars in an instant? Probably not. From a human perspective, the only way that all things are possible is through our imagination. Our imagination is completely unrestricted, unlimited, and infinite. In our imagination, we can do anything, making it a powerful spiritual tool for manifesting.

The key to harnessing the power of our imagination is to focus on feeling. *Feel* yourself having, doing, or being whatever the thing is you desire. When we mentally claim our desires and lose ourselves in the feeling of being the thing we desire, the quality or experience will embody itself in our world. This is how Spiritual Law works.

Imagine the full scene of your desire already completed in your mind. For instance, if there is a goal you want to accomplish, imagine someone you know congratulating you on your task. Hear their words complimenting you, telling you, "Great job!" Feel their handshake or hug. Make it so real in your imagination that you feel a response in your body—feel it as if you are in that moment of accomplishment. This is how we manifest our dreams.

Affirm

*I know all things are possible,
and I know it all starts in my imagination.*

PERSPECTIVE IS EVERYTHING
OCTOBER 22

When we stand on the earth facing east in the early morning, we watch the sun rise. At the end of the day, we face west and watch the beauty of a sunset. In reality, the sun is neither rising nor setting. The earth is what is actually moving. When you lie on your back outside on the ground and look up at the stars at night, sometimes you can get a sense of our planet's rotation. If you concentrate hard enough, you can feel the subtle yet compelling movement. It is a powerful shift in perspective to think and feel this way. The same is true for other areas of our lives. It only takes our concentration and awareness to shift our perspective.

What if we saw our problems and troubles as valuable lessons and gentle nudges from Spirit? Viewing them positively can create just the shift we need to clear obstacles, manifest change, and experience the life we desire.

Affirm

My problems are only lessons,
and I can always create the life I desire.

HOW TO PREDICT THE FUTURE
OCTOBER 23

We like to predict our future based on our past experience. Sometimes this is very helpful. For example, if you touch a hot stove and get burned, you remember next time not to touch the hot stove. Sometimes, though, humans apply this concept a little too harshly.

Imagine if you had a romantic relationship where the person you dated ended up being a real jerk. You ended the relationship and walked away with the memory of that negative experience. If you take that experience and then predict your future based on it, you will think and believe that anyone you start dating will behave in exactly the same way. You would be expecting any new relationship to fail without even giving it a chance. That is no way to live your life!

Expectation based on our negative false beliefs causes us to repeat those patterns that originally created the negative experience. It eliminates the element of possibility and knocks us out of alignment with the Divine Truth that all things are possible, including good and positive things. Are you consciously aware of what you are thinking and expecting to happen? Are you clinging to negative past experiences and letting them influence your beliefs?

Affirm

*No matter what happened in the past, good,
positive experiences are always possible for me!*

CHOOSE AWARENESS
OCTOBER 24

Spiritual awareness doesn't always happen overnight. Sometimes it begins as a small, shaky willingness to express what is true, even when the world feels frightening, unstable, and out of control. We live in times marked by war, corruption, injustice, and uncertainty. It can feel overwhelming to try to stay spiritually awake in the middle of it all.

We don't wait for perfect conditions to live consciously. We practice awareness in the middle of real life—while watching disturbing headlines, navigating systems that seem broken, worrying about our loved ones, or wondering what kind of world we are leaving behind. We might wonder if our efforts even matter. Rest assured that your effort itself is holy. The willingness to stay present and keep choosing awareness when fear would be easier is our spiritual work.

This work isn't about self-mastery or getting it right. It's about our devotion to awareness. Even when our expression feels imperfect, something real is moving through us. That movement is God expressing as you. Not someday in the future. Not when the world calms down. Right now.

We don't always know if what we offer is beautiful, powerful, effective, or impactful, but we can trust that choosing awareness, choosing love, and doing our best to live in Truth—especially in uncertain times—is truly God in action.

Affirm

*Today and every day,
I make the effort to consciously choose spiritual awareness.*

PEACE OF MIND
OCTOBER 25

Got problems? Most people do!

Maybe our problems don't actually need to be fixed. Maybe it's just our thoughts about our problems that need fixing. We know our attitude, disposition, and outlook influence our outcomes and life experience. Which is more important? That your problems be fixed, or that you have the peace of mind to live life unbothered by any possible difficulty that arises?

Peace of mind is both empowering and freeing. It is also available to you at any given moment, no matter what circumstance you find yourself experiencing. You are the one who has a choice about how you relate to, interact with, and show up in the world. It is amazing how many problems get solved when we stop believing in problems to begin with. How do you want to be in this world? Decide today to walk in the full awareness that no change, problem, or perceived bad situation can threaten your inner stability and spiritual awareness.

Affirm

Today, I choose to walk in spiritual awareness,
embracing the peace of mind that comes with knowing all is well.

DEMAND IT. BELIEVE IT. EXPECT IT
OCTOBER 26

What do you do if you are in a situation where you are disappointed, frustrated, or upset? Try this. Say, "I demand to see the good in this."

That's it. You don't have to do anything more. You put the demand on Spirit (or whatever you call it, God, Spirit, Universe, Source, Infinite Intelligence, etc.) that you wish to see the good in this difficult situation. *You* don't have to find the good because you have left that up to Spirit. All you have to do is believe it is there. How could there possibly be any good in whatever you are facing? If you believe there is good, and you demand to see it, then trust and wait for it to be revealed.

The catch is, you actually have to believe there is good in there somewhere, no matter how ugly the situation is. Believe that there is good and fully expect to see it. Hold that expectation and watch the good appear.

Affirm

I demand to see the good in this!
I believe there is good, and I fully expect to see it.

PAUSE FOR GUIDANCE
OCTOBER 27

Before satellites, GPS map apps, and cellphone service, a road trip journey meant unfolding a big, folded paper map or getting out an atlas to help navigate your way. Nowadays, we pause for just a moment to put our destination into our cellphones' GPS before we hit the road. We let an app guide us, turn by turn, which way to go. It helps us avoid traffic, accidents, and construction. Wouldn't it be nice to do this spiritually as we navigate our life situations?

It just takes a moment to pause and receive the guidance we need. It's about being still long enough to become conscious of the still small voice inside that guides us. We receive that which we are conscious of. Believing in this guiding force permits us to access more of it. Set reminders throughout the day to pause and check your guidance system, the Divine within you.

Affirm

*My connection to the Divine Spirit, my Guiding Positioning System,
is what keeps me on track in my life.
The signal is clear, and I am listening.*

PREPARE TO BE WOWED!
OCTOBER 28

Just when I think I have captured the most beautiful sunset, I come back the next day, and that sunset seems to say to me, "Let me see what I can do for you!" It's magnificent. That is what life is like. We always have the opportunity to look for the beauty and look for our good. We can give the Divine the opportunity to wow and amaze us daily. It only takes our attention and our awareness. Our good is revealed when we actively, expectantly look for it.

It doesn't matter what we call It—God, Spirit, Universe, Source, Infinite Intelligence, or just the Divine. We can always be open and willing to be wowed. What are you looking for today? Look for your good… because it's there, just waiting for your attention.

Affirm

Today, I am committed to seeking, finding, and enjoying my good.
All of God's great good is available to me in this moment.

OPPORTUNITY FOR TRANSFORMATION
OCTOBER 29

Your life experiences are a reflection of your consciousness. If things are a mess, your consciousness might be a mess. God does not wish for you to live with problems, instability, abuse, disease, unhappiness, pain, or suffering. These things are simply indicators that we may need to spend some time going within, trusting, learning, studying, meditating, praying, and seeking to be in alignment with the Divine. When we are living in alignment, we simply don't have the problems we had before.

To be clear, this is never taught from a place of judgment. It comes from a place of great responsibility and opportunity. If your life feels like it's a mess, you can fix it! You get to create your own transformation.

Affirm

Every moment I am focused on God
is another step toward living a balanced, easy life.

A HEALING METHOD
OCTOBER 30

In the late 1800s, Myrtle Fillmore, who, with her husband Charles, started Unity Church, needed to heal her physical body. One of the things she did was talk to her organs. She told her body the Truth using words of strength and power. The Truth of your body, of any organ, any body system, is that it is spiritually perfect and divinely made. Illness and disease are not the Truth of your physical body's expression. Talking to her body was part of Myrtle's method of healing, and it worked.

This method is available to you, too. You can talk to your body and remind it of spiritual Truth. Your body deserves and desires your attention. When you speak to it lovingly and envision it thriving with health and wholeness, Spiritual Law has no alternative but to respond. You can actively take part in your physical healing, no matter what the human appearances look like. This is how we heal.

Affirm

Today, I talk to my organs, and I actively take part in my body's ability to express as perfect wholeness.

NO VEIL
OCTOBER 31

"The veil is thin" is a saying frequently heard around Halloween, the Day of the Dead, and All Saints' Day. But what if the veil really isn't thin? What if the veil doesn't exist at all? What if there is no separation between people who are alive, existing in a physical body on earth, and people who have transitioned?

Consider that human beings can only hear sounds with frequencies within a certain range, but there are most certainly sounds that occur beyond that range. Likewise, the visible light frequencies that humans can perceive are only a small portion of the spectrum of possible wavelengths. There is more out there than we can see, hear, and sense. What if our loved ones are closer than we think?

If we believe that life is eternal, which almost every religion and faith tradition teaches, then there really is no separation between this realm of being and the spiritual realm. There is only Being, no matter how we are expressing. There is not this side or that side. It is all one. It is comforting to believe life is eternal and there is no veil. Any thought of separation comes from our own lack of understanding and maybe our own unwillingness to see life as truly one continuous experience.

Affirm

*Today, I remain open to the idea
that all life is one and eternal.*

NOVEMBER

YOU CAN'T TAKE THAT AWAY FROM ME
NOVEMBER 1

When you go in person to apply for a passport, a government official takes your photo. There are rules for the photo. It must be a certain size. The background has to be white or off white. You can't wear a uniform, hat, or glasses. And the worst rule is, you aren't allowed to smile because smiling and showing teeth in particular makes it difficult for facial recognition tools to confirm your identity.

When I went through this process, the postal worker handling my application took his job quite seriously, collecting and checking all my official documents meticulously. When it came time for him to take my photo, he instructed me where to stand and told me, "No having fun. No smiling!" He wasn't joking. I thought this must be the saddest part of his job, to literally take away people's joy, however temporarily.

Fortunately, this no-smiling rule only applies to passport photos, not life in general. I am going to continue having fun and smiling no matter what happens. No government policy can take away our right to joy. It is innate. It is our divine nature. Shine your light. Laugh. Smile.

Affirm

Today, I make a conscious effort to smile as much as possible.
I express as joy, and I see it everywhere!

MAKE IT A GAME
NOVEMBER 2

Improve your manifestation abilities and skills with this fun game. Every night, before you go to bed, ask yourself questions like: What was the best part of my day? What was my favorite thing that happened? What am I most grateful for today?

When you play this game every night, it trains you to shift your attention to your good—whatever good thing you experienced, whatever made you happy, whatever was fun. When we shift our attention to our good, remember, the Universe is saying *yes* to that. You will gain more good things to choose from each day.

What do we typically do instead of this game when we get into bed? Unfortunately, we think about all the negative things that might have happened that day. The stupid meeting you had to attend for work, the jerk who cut you off for the parking spot at the grocery store, the fight you had with your sister on the phone, etc. We always seem to rehash the bad things that happened during the day. Not anymore!

Now, play this new game to shift your focus. Focusing on the good is like a muscle. You are training your manifestation skills and actively working on your ability to stay focused on your good so that you end up attracting more to you.

Ask

What was the best part of my day?

NO RESISTING
NOVEMBER 3

A phrase attributed to psychologist Carl Jung says, "That which you resist, persists." In other words, fighting against something is not going to get rid of it. For example, back in the 1980s, there was a campaign against drug use called the "War on Drugs." It did not get rid of the drug problem in America by any means. There is a "Fight Against Breast Cancer" campaign, which seems equally inefficient in stopping the disease. Being against something, fighting a war against it, opposing it with our words, doesn't get rid of it. Why? Because it brings the battle to the forefront of our minds. It pushes us to focus our attention on the problem that we don't want to experience. It puts our consciousness in a state of resistance.

What happens when we shift our thinking and decide instead to be *for* something? Consider these questions: What are you for? Are you for sobriety and clean living? Are you for health and wholeness? Those positive options are more powerful than fighting against something, and they are a different way to think about things that are not so great in this world, like a drug problem, cancer, and disease. This works on a personal and collective level, too. What can you be *for* in your life? Funnel your attention toward what you want to experience instead of the problem. It is a more powerful approach to manifestation and spiritual well-being as well as a more effective way to bring about the changes we want to see.

Ask

What am I for in my life?

IT'S ABOUT US
NOVEMBER 4

An invocation is a prayer that invokes, invites, and calls upon God, often said before a public event. We know the Truth that God is not separate from us, waiting for an invitation to come near. On the contrary, God is Omnipresence, always present in all ways, at all times. An invocation doesn't really have anything to do with God. It has to do with us. What an invocation does is shifts our awareness, so we recognize God's presence in the moment. We are not invoking God; we are invoking our awareness of God. This process can certainly happen at times other than public events.

You can, at any given moment, go within to think or say your own invocation. There is no limit to the number of times you can shift your awareness to the Divine. Why not use this moment right now?

Affirm

*In this moment, I turn within and know the Truth
that there is One Power, One Presence, One Life back of all things.
I shift my awareness to this reality,
knowing I am united fully with this One Life.
It is my life!*

WHAT DO YOU WANT?
NOVEMBER 5

At a spiritual retreat, participants were paired up to do an exercise. A timer was set for ninety seconds. One partner was to look into the eyes of the other and ask, "What do you want?" repeatedly until the timer went off. The other partner was to answer the question out loud, with legitimate answers each time. You could say anything. The dialogue might go like this:

"What do you want?"   *"I want world peace."*
"What do you want?"   *"I want a turkey sandwich."*
"What do you want?"   *"I want to be loved."*
"What do you want?"   *"I want to get married."*
"What do you want?"   *"I want more money."*
"What do you want?"   *"I want to know God."*
"What do you want?"   *"I want to stop drinking."*
"What do you want?"   *"I want my brother to love me."*

You had to keep responding, digging deep in your heart to discover what it was you truly wanted. Sometimes it was challenging to think of something to say, but you had to keep answering. After ninety-seconds, the partners switched roles and did it again. It was powerfully moving.

This exercise can also be done alone. Set a timer, record a voice memo, or write down your answers. Things may come up that you didn't even realize you wanted. *This* is clarity.

Ask

What do I want?

TRIGGER QUESTIONS
NOVEMBER 6

We know that repressed emotions, lack of forgiveness, and anger can all contribute to symptoms, illness, and disease. When our mind is experiencing disharmony, we can manifest that disharmony in our body. When you experience physical symptoms and aren't feeling well, instead of asking yourself, "What's the matter with me?" ask yourself, "*Who's* the matter with me?" The question may trigger a response that helps explain what is happening metaphysically in your body. Perhaps there is someone you need to forgive, a relationship that needs addressing, or emotions that need releasing.

Similarly, the root cause of pain and illness is often repressed anger. Other questions that can trigger an insightful response are "Who am I angry at?" or "What am I angry about?" Working through our emotions, thoughts, and feelings helps us to maintain a healthy, balanced life.

Ask

Who am I angry at?
What am I angry about?
What triggered this feeling?
Do I have forgiveness to practice?

GLIMPSE THE ONENESS
NOVEMBER 7

We can spend years studying the Truth that we are one—the Truth of our unity as humanity. We hear this, and we think, *How beautiful! What a lovely thought!* And then we look around. We look at our neighbors and our family. We look at the news and what is going on in the world, and we realize the farce of it all. We're certainly not acting like we are all one!

Imagine a hand with the palm facing up, fingers pointing to the sky. This hand is under the ground. All you see is the individual fingers above the ground. The fingers represent people, each one of us. The palm and wrist parts of the hand underground are the Universe (God, Spirit, whatever you call it). It is one entity. One being—*the* Being. When we see the individual fingers, it looks like we are all separate, but really, we are all one.

For the sake of humanity, it is crucial that we understand the Truth of our oneness and unity. We must seek out all the ways this concept is driven home for us, so we can live it and believe it.

Affirm

*We are all expressions of the One Universal Life.
We are ONE.*

SPIRITUAL JOURNEY
NOVEMBER 8

Consider these questions about how far you have come on your spiritual journey:

What did you believe about God when you were ten years old?
How about as a teenager or young adult?
How about now?
Did God change, or did your understanding change?

We know God is changeless, so the truth is, you have grown in your spiritual understanding of God. It wasn't that you were dumb as a child. Your faith and understanding have simply further developed because of your spiritual journey.

Are you actively participating in your spiritual journey?
Are you willing to make more leaps and allow your beliefs to change?

Affirm

I am always willing to learn and grow in my spiritual understanding.
My beliefs about God are always changing
in ways that positively influence my life experience.

START AT THE BEGINNING
NOVEMBER 9

Sometimes, a positive affirmation feels like you are lying to yourself. Every day you might affirm things like: "Everything is okay. I am abundant. I am healthy. I am loved, etc." But the words don't feel true. It doesn't mean you have failed; it's just a signal to return to the beginning.

Sometimes we have to go back to the feelings that motivated us to start our spiritual journey in the first place, back to the thoughts that moved us to begin using affirmations. Sometimes spiritual growth happens through our patience and old fashioned repetition. We keep trying. We keep thinking new thoughts. We do the practice, even when our beliefs have not yet caught up.

If you struggle with affirmations, these are some new simple ones to try. Remember that progress is happening, even when it feels slow.

Affirm

I am willing to change my thought patterns.
I am doing my best.
I am learning to do better.
I am open to receiving spiritual guidance.
I am bravely exploring my spiritual nature.
I am discovering how to love myself.
I love myself enough to affirm my Truth.

FOUR LITTLE WORDS
NOVEMBER 10

We set goals, make intentions, speak declarations, meditate, visualize, and pray. We have all kinds of plans for our lives and wish to manifest all kinds of things. We do the necessary spiritual work to co-create with Spirit and receive demonstrations. But we never want to place a limit on Spirit. These four little words are very important: *This or something better.*

If we really want $10,000 in our bank account, we certainly don't want to tell Spirit that is all we are willing to accept. We might want a new car, thinking a little used hatchback compact car would suffice and meet our needs, fully rejecting a brand new luxury sport utility vehicle that might be available to us. When you make your intentions known to Spirit, complete your request with "this or something better," trusting Spirit knows best and will bring you exactly what you need.

We don't tell Spirit how or what to manifest. We needn't be concerned with the specifics or the details. Always be willing to accept far beyond your wildest dreams.

Affirm

Today, I allow Spirit the opportunity to wow and impress me.

KEEP THE FAITH
NOVEMBER 11

What are some things you accept in faith? What do you accept without physical evidence or proof? When you drive over a bridge, you have full faith in its ability to support your vehicle, but the truth is, bridges can collapse. You accept a chair will hold you up when you sit in it, but occasionally, chairs break. Many people travel on airplanes thousands of feet in the air, with full faith that they will reach their destination safely, but rarely, on tragic occasions, airplanes crash. You go to sleep each night, having full faith that tomorrow the sun will rise, trusting you will wake up in the morning to a brand new day, but unfortunately, sometimes, people die in their sleep.

In some of these examples, we don't even give any thought to them. We go on about our lives, driving over the bridge, plopping into the chair, getting on the plane, and going to sleep. These are all good things human beings have faith in, believe in, and accept as truth. If we can't accept things in faith, we would be doomed to a life filled with doubt, and that is no way to live. Think of the fearful level of neurosis we would all experience if we didn't put our faith in something good. Living faithfully is a better way to live.

Affirm

Today, I choose to exercise my faith and believe in the good.

HIGHER SELF
NOVEMBER 12

What is your higher self? You have heard it is best to live in alignment with your "higher self" or what a good idea it is to get in touch with your "higher self." Who is that? What does that even mean?

Your higher self is the part of you that knows your Truth. It knows you are divine, and you have a divine nature. It knows you express as all the qualities and traits of the Divine. You are Abundance. You are Divine Love. You are Creativity. You are Intelligence. You are Wisdom. You are Harmony. You have this capability within you to express as Wholeness, Health, and Wellness. Being in touch with your higher self is knowing this Truth and knowing it so well that you live from that perspective. When you do this, your actual life–the things around you, your situations, your circumstances–can't help but reflect this Truth back to you.

Affirm

*I am in touch with my higher self,
creating the life I desire and deserve.*

MAKE IT A HABIT
NOVEMBER 13

Motivation may be what gets us started, but habit is what keeps us going. This idea is often applied to exercise routines, but it can apply to anything in life: exercise, diet, sobriety, even habits like meditation, prayer, and spiritual study.

What motivates you to pay attention to your spiritual journey?

What prompts you to participate in spiritual practice and seek a relationship with the Divine?

How have these practices become habits for you?

Has reading the entries in this book become a daily habit?

Why is it important for humans to habitually shift their attention to their spiritual awareness?

Affirm

Every day I am motivated to learn and grow spiritually.
It is my habit to remind myself of the Truth.

YOU ARE BEING USED
NOVEMBER 14

A New Thought tenant suggests, there is a power for good in the universe, greater than any one person, and it is always active. Yet, we look around, and it seems like very few people are using this great spiritual power for good. We see greed, selfishness, aggression, misery, and pain. This power, this Spiritual Law of Life, responds to our thought and always says yes. It is automatic and exact. It is carrying out whatever is put into it.

Perhaps the idea needs to be turned around to suggest, there is a power for good in the universe, and it is using you. Good or bad, the One Power of Spirit *creates*. It is Its very nature to listen, respond, and create. Are you paying attention to what It is doing? What is It creating through you? What is It using your life to create and do in this world? You can participate in this great Creative Process.

Shift your awareness and harness the power of your thoughts, beliefs, and actions.

Affirm

I am more powerful than I think.

THE CLUB FOR ALL THINGS
NOVEMBER 15

There is a joke that goes:

Q: What do you call a book club that gets stuck on the same book forever?
A: Church.

There is some stinging truth in the joke. It would be limiting and restricting for a book club to be stuck on the same book forever—it wouldn't work. If we viewed church as a book club, we would, of course, acknowledge that the Bible is a tremendous book of deep spiritual wisdom. We could also recognize that there are a lot of other great books, too!

One could argue that to be truly spiritually aware, open, inclusive, evolved, and united, we need to be exposed to all the things. All the books. All the faith traditions. All the rituals. All the insights. We need all the new ideas that everyone brings, all the ways that we connect with the Divine. *That's* the ultimate book club. That's the club we can choose to be in, where we discover various methods to access and experience the Divine. That's how we realize our oneness.

Affirm

I am free to read all the books, do all the rituals,
and receive all the insights that support me on my spiritual journey.

YOU DESERVE BETTER
NOVEMBER 16

When my children were young, I struggled as a single mother. There were things in our house that were broken for a long time. I was not mechanically inclined, and there was no extra money to hire professionals to get things fixed. For instance, when I started dating the man who became my husband, our kitchen sink's garbage disposal had been broken for over a year. We all just knew not to use that side of the sink because it was broken. He came along and fixed it in a matter of minutes. He was very handy, mechanically inclined, and knew exactly what to do.

My children and I had the mentality and consciousness of living with broken things. It became our family joke, saying things like, "Oh, we step over that broken tile," or "We don't use that shower." Our mentality was to accept things as broken and just live that way. It is a level of consciousness—to be in a state of accepting broken things around you as if that is what you deserve. The truth, of course, was that we deserved to live in a home where things were not broken. But we had to come to that realization.

Do you have this realization? Not being able to afford repairs and not knowing how to do them for yourself are valid human issues to deal with, but first, you have to make sure that in your consciousness, you understand and believe you deserve abundance, that you deserve to live in a perfectly wonderful, functioning home that supports you. Once you fix this mindset, you start to see things shift all around you.

Act

Believe in and accept the good you deserve.

WHAT IS F.E.A.R.?
NOVEMBER 17

Years ago, in my "Foundations of The Science of Mind and Spirit" class, the practitioner teacher gave us an acronym for the word fear. She told us that F.E.A.R. is just "Forgetting. Everything's. All. Right." What that acronym does is shifts your attention away from the circumstance, away from the human condition that is causing you to feel fear, and it shifts it to your spiritual Truth that nothing can harm you, that all is well, that God is present always, in all ways.

Virtually every human "problem" can be boiled down to the root cause of fear. Fear of lack, fear of disease, fear of death, fear of loneliness, fear of looking foolish, etc. One might think the way to avoid fear is to act from its opposite—to react and respond with bravery and courage. The problem with this is that courage is not the opposite of fear. You can be courageous and still feel afraid!

I believe the opposite of fear is whatever the God quality is that we are seeking in the moment. If we remember "everything is all right," then that means we are filled with a sense of abundance, life, love, joy, peace, etc.—whatever Truth we need to realize. This is the state of consciousness that eliminates all fear.

Affirm

*Today, I release my fear
and put my faith fully in God's Omnipresence.
All is well.*

HOW ARE YOU DOING?
NOVEMBER 18

During the COVID-19 pandemic back in 2020, the late beloved actor Leslie Jordan went viral for his Instagram account reels that typically began with "How y'all doin'?" His videos perfectly demonstrated the power of the "check-in." So many people were feeling isolated from their friends, family members, and community at that time. The check-in wasn't just for comedy's sake. It pushed us to check in with ourselves, our true selves. It made us think about and ask ourselves how we were really doing.

The check-in was a moment of mindfulness and an opportunity to practice spiritual awareness. Just because the pandemic has (thankfully) ended, doesn't mean we can't still use practices like this. These mindful check-ins are tremendously helpful. Yes, we can continue to check in with our loved ones and others, but we can also check in with our true self.

Ask

How am I doing? How is my soul?
How is my higher self?
Does it feel grounded? Connected? Whole?
Does it need attention? More stillness? More joy?

A LITTLE STRESS
NOVEMBER 19

The Biosphere 2 at the University of Arizona is the world's largest controlled environment dedicated to understanding climate change. The giant 3.14-acre laboratory perfectly replicates earth conditions for water, desert, plants, trees, etc.

Scientists noticed that the trees grew rapidly in the pefect conditions, but did not mature at the same rate. They were falling over. Why? Because wind was missing in this perfect environment. Trees need wind. They need the resistance of the wind to be able to strengthen their roots and be grounded. That stress of the wind resistance is actually beneficial to their growth, resilience, and ultimately their quality of life.

What if this is true for all life, including humans? Perhaps some stress is good for us. Afterall, when we resist something, it causes us to be grounded in our roots—the Truth of who we are. We need "good stress," the resistance to knock us off balance a little bit to make us remember who we are. A little stress is okay if it strengthens our faith. The question is, how much stress? A gentle breeze might be so soft we don't notice it. A hurricane-force wind could knock us flat on our backs.

A little stress can be good. When you fear the things happening in the world, and you want to resist what you are seeing, maybe there is some good to be found in that situation. Are you remembering the Truth of who you are?

Affirm

Stress is an opportunity to get grounded, check out my roots, and remember my spiritual Truth.

MAKE A NOTE
NOVEMBER 20

The Notes app on your phone is a handy tool for jotting down things you want to remember, like grocery lists, recipes, important information, appointments, etc. You can even share access to your notes with family members or friends. Did you know this tool can also be used as a way to increase your awareness of your good and help you stay in a state of gratitude?

Open a new note on your phone and title it: "Good Things Are Always Happening." At some point during your day make a point to add something to the list. Soon, you will have a great gratitude list of so many good things that have happened to you. It's such a simple way to shift our attention, our focus, and our awareness to our good.

Affirm

Good things are always happening to me!

YOUR PEACE MATTERS
NOVEMBER 21

There are so many things to be outraged about today. That is why it is so important to prioritize your peace. Your peace matters. When you find yourself getting outraged about something, you feel it in your body. You feel tension, anger, racing thoughts, and upset. Can you identify that feeling? When we notice what we are feeling in our body, we can make the effort to counteract it with the question: What can I do in this moment to restore myself to peace?

It might look like choosing to take a few deep breaths, going to meditate for a while, or finding something that makes you laugh. It is making the choice to serve yourself and cater to your higher self, your soul. Take a moment to remember the Truth of who and what you are—a child of the Divine. Do whatever it takes for you to experience peace and joy.

Affirm

Today, I commit to prioritizing my peace.

TURN IT OFF
NOVEMBER 22

Have you ever lost your cell phone? Panic unfolds. You feel lost and disconnected, like you've left part of yourself behind. The fear and anxiety that follows is a normal human reaction, but it begs the question: Who are we without our phones? Who are we without access to our apps, our social media profiles, our contact lists, and our text messages? There is so much data about us stored on our cell phones and in our daily internet activity. We are more than our data. Everything about you on your cell phone is about the human ego-based you. Your cell phone knows:

- Who you talk to, FaceTime, text, and email
- Where you shop
- What you take photos of
- What is on your grocery list
- What e-books you read
- Which social media apps you use
- How many points you have at which coffee shop
- How good you are at a daily word game
- Which online videos you like to watch
- What your bank account balance is

But, does your phone say anything about who you *really* are? Challenge yourself. Turn off the phone for a moment. Who are you?

Affirm

I am a child of the Divine. Perfect, whole, and complete.
Nothing can separate me from my Divine Truth.

A STATE OF BALANCE
NOVEMBER 23

Houses have thermostats that regulate their temperature. You set the desired temperature you want. You are in control. The thermostat does the work to automatically turn on the heat or air conditioning if the temperature falls below or goes above the temperature you set. It maintains perfect balance because that is what it is designed to do. Once it is set correctly, we don't need to give it any thought. It comes on and goes off when we need it.

The human body operates in a similar way. Multiple organs and body systems constantly work to maintain homeostasis—our body's ability to remain stable internally, even when external conditions change. It happens automatically. We don't give much thought to this because thankfully, it happens without our effort and without us even noticing. But who set the temperature to your "internal thermostat"? Divine Intelligence did because life operates in a state of balance. This is your Truth.

Affirm

My natural state of being is stable and balanced.

TOM THE TURKEY'S MESSAGE
NOVEMBER 24

Many people decorate their homes for holidays. You see hearts in windows around Valentine's Day, spooky ghosts and witches in front yards around Halloween, and lights on houses for those who celebrate Christmas. Year after year, folks put away the scary stuff in early November and immediately drag out the Santa Claus and string lights. Thanksgiving is often skipped right over—with no decorations put out.

My yard has a six-foot-tall inflatable light-up turkey in it. He holds a sign that says, "GIVE THANKS!" It's silly and obnoxious and often gets blown over on blustery November days. I insist on decorating for Thanksgiving because gratitude is a spiritual principle that makes a powerful difference in our individual lives and in the world. What if just one person sees my ridiculous turkey, laughs at it, reads the sign, and then pauses to give thanks for all the good in their life? That's enough for me! Gratitude matters. Spread the word.

Affirm

Today, and every day, I give thanks.

"WE INTERRUPT THIS PROGRAM..."
NOVEMBER 25

There is tremendous power in the pattern interrupt. If you are trying to solve a problem, or are stuck in a pattern of destructive behavior or negative thoughts, DO SOMETHING DIFFERENT. Distract yourself. Go for a walk. Drive a different way to work. Rearrange the furniture in your house. Pick out a book you would not normally read. Strike up a conversation with a stranger. Travel to a city you have never visited. Do something—anything—out of the ordinary.

When we interrupt our regular pattern of thought, it forces us to think something new. It's not really about us, though. This process allows Spirit the opportunity to work. Creative insights, revelations, and realizations happen when we are jolted out of our old habits and old patterns of thought. Change things up. Give God the opportunity to inspire you and reveal your good.

Affirm

*It is safe to do something different
and interrupt my old patterns of thought.*

YOU'VE GOT POTENTIAL
NOVEMBER 26

You've heard the idea of "living up to your potential." It means to live your best life, to the best of your abilities, fully expressing and using all your talents, always being willing to grow and improve yourself. But what about living up to our spiritual potential?

Our spiritual potential is in God—or whatever you call the One Power, One Presence of all life. Our potential is perfect in God, therefore, within us is the potential of all good and perfect experience. The Bible tells us that it is the Father's good pleasure to give us the kingdom. That means that we have the potential in every given moment to receive and experience all God's goodness. Our spiritual potential is realized as we become willing participants in our relationship with the Divine. We live up to this spiritual potential when we consciously turn toward God with our attention, awareness, and practice, allowing ourselves to receive what is ours by birthright.

Ask

What great potential is inside me, waiting to express?

BE LIKE A BISON
NOVEMBER 27

Bison are beautiful, majestic animals that thrive in both freezing cold temperatures and stifling hot weather. They have an interesting characteristic that makes them behave differently than other herded farm animals like cattle, goats, sheep, and horses. Bison will turn directly into a snowstorm instead of drifting with the wind because they instinctively know that heading toward the storm will get them out of the bad weather faster. Their giant heads act like a snowplow. They swing them back and forth, head down, focused and intent on moving forward.

This is a fascinating metaphor for humans dealing with the storms of life. When we find ourselves in difficult situations, it behooves us to confront it head on, stay focused on our spiritual Truth, and keep moving forward. It does not benefit us to drift aimlessly with the wind, prolonging our suffering while we try to outrun our problems. When we know our spiritual Truth, we are empowered and steadfast. Never underestimate your faith.

Affirm

I trust what awaits me on the other side of my troubles.

AT THE MOVIES
NOVEMBER 28

When we go to the movies, we are an objective third party, watching a story on the screen. We can see things happening that the characters don't seem to know or understand. Sometimes, we can clearly tell what's coming next. We want to yell at the people on screen—give them a warning, tell them to avoid a pitfall, suggest they focus on something else, make them do something to improve their outcome. If they could just listen to us, their story would be so much simpler, easier, and better!

Can you shift your awareness out of your own story for a moment? Ask for guidance, clarity, and answers. Take these questions to meditation.

Ask

If my life were a movie, what would the audience be yelling at the screen?
What would an objective third-party person
who is watching my life unfold tell me to do right now
for me to live my best life and experience my highest good?

A BETTER WAY
NOVEMBER 29

Sometimes, when we look at all the chaos and discord in the world, we feel disappointed, frustrated, and uncomfortable. There is a reason for this. You are uncomfortable because you know that a better reality is possible. You are spiritually aware. You know the Truth of our unity and oneness. You know peace is possible, and humans are choosing not to exist in peace. It wouldn't bother you if you didn't know deep down what is possible.

Perhaps chaos is the tool capital-L-Life is using to push us to recognize and realize the Truth of our unity. In the midst of the chaos, we can use our discomfort to do just that. Remember, there is freedom in knowing how bad a situation really is, so that we may mindfully choose something better.

There is a plan. There is a better way. Choose to believe in it. Live from it.

Affirm

I choose to use my discomfort as a reminder that there is a better way.

YOUR NEEDS FIRST
NOVEMBER 30

When a family travels on an airplane with an infant, the flight attendant always tells the parents, "If there is a change in cabin pressure, and the oxygen masks come down, put your own mask on first, then put on your child's mask." The truth is, if you tried to put your child's mask on first, you might pass out and not finish! The flight crew must make a point to give parents this instruction because it goes against human nature to be selfish and put your own needs above your child's. It is counterintuitive as a parent, but in that situation, it is necessary for the good of your survival. Your decision to focus on yourself ultimately causes the good outcome of your safety—both yours and your child's.

We can look at the collective consciousness the same way. To be a positive shining light in the world, you must focus on your own higher self. It is the strength of your own faith, your own connection with Source, your own ability to be grounded and aware of God-consciousness that helps lift the consciousness of the world. Take care of your own spiritual needs first. It causes a ripple effect of goodness that emanates into the world.

Affirm

Focusing on my spiritual life makes a difference in the world.

DECEMBER

BRING THE LIGHT
DECEMBER 1

Every year, after daylight savings time ends, the darkness reminds us how much we need the light. The dark days of early December lead up to the hopeful celebrations of the winter solstice, Hanukkah, Christmas, and Kwanzaa. We find ourselves decorating and putting up lights at this time of year in our homes, taking the time to drag out the boxes, making the effort to unravel all the knotted strings of lights, and even going to the store for new lights if necessary. We climb up the ladder to hang and arrange everything just right.

None of the decorating, none of the "light bringing" happens without *us*. We must make the effort. We are the "light bringers" for Spirit. We do the "shining" because just like the upcoming solstice demonstrates, darkness cannot overtake the world. Nothing can dim the Spirit within you. You bring the light to the world this time of year. Shine bright.

Affirm

I am the Light of God.
I shine my light today and always.

DECEMBER SELF-LOVE
DECEMBER 2

The month of December is in the thick of the holiday season. Use today's entry as a reminder to be gentle with yourself during the holidays. It may sound silly, because holidays are wonderful, right? There is so much joy and love, but the older we get, the more we realize this is not always the case. It is important for us to be gentle with ourselves, with the expectations we might have, the hectic nature of holiday events, the potential for financial strain, grief and loss we might be experiencing, etc. December can be a hard month. Take these words as your gift of permission.

If you need to "feel the feels" and go sit and cry, do that. If you need to set boundaries and say no to excessive commitments, do that. If you need to decline buying gifts, doing the holiday baking, decorating the house this year, do that. Give yourself the self-care you need—whatever it is. You matter.

Affirm

*I love and support myself fully
during the month of December and always.*

GET YOURSELF GOING
DECEMBER 3

An exercise video began with the message, "This is the workout to do when you are feeling lazy and don't want to work out. Don't worry, the music will make you want to get up and move!" I was intrigued. It turns out the instructor was right. The music did make me want to get up and move. It was upbeat and inspiring. I started with a tired, lazy, uninterested attitude, and then the next thing I knew, I was up and exercising like a champ.

What about when we are feeling spiritually lazy, and don't want to do the work to acknowledge and build up our faith? Who says you have to invest hours of time and energy in your spiritual life? Make it easy on yourself. There are so many social media accounts that share inspirational snippets of spiritual wisdom. There are apps that send you mantras, affirmations, and inspirational quotes. Short daily readings of ancient wisdom texts or contemporary spiritual writing like those found in this book can be just what we need to inspire us, spark our enthusiasm, and reignite our faith.

Affirm

I let short bursts of inspirational material inspire me throughout the day.

HONOR THEM
DECEMBER 4

Once a woman was walking to her car in a parking lot a few days before Christmas. It was cold, and she was tired of shopping. A stranger approached her, handed her what looked like a Christmas card in an envelope, and said, "Merry Christmas!" Then the stranger quickly walked away. When she opened it, it wasn't a Christmas card. It was a picture of a man she did not know. Under the picture, it said:

"This is my father, John. This will be our first Christmas without him. He was a shining light in our family, and we all miss him very much. He taught us to always be kind and generous. We miss buying him his Christmas gift. Please accept this gift card in his memory. Blessings of love and light to you and your family."

The true story illustrates a uniquely touching way to honor a loved one and spread kindness to humanity.

Ask

In what ways do I honor my loved ones who have transitioned?

THE WALK-AWAY STRATEGY
DECEMBER 5

Have you ever had a problem that you couldn't seem to solve, whether at work, with your hobby, or some life situation? When we are stuck and can't seem to figure something out, it is important to be spiritually aware, have faith, and trust in our oneness with the One Mind. In fact, trusting is crucial. When we say, affirm, and declare: "There is One Mind—that Mind is God, and that mind is my mind now," we are speaking a Truth we can trust in. We don't have to spin our wheels, get frustrated, fight, or struggle in our human problems. We can put the problem down... and walk away.

Albert Einstein once said, "I think ninety-nine times and find nothing. I stop thinking, swim in the silence, and the truth comes to me." In other words, he stopped working and stopped thinking about his problem altogether. Instead, he walked away and did something else—something in the silence. Maybe he went off to meditate. Maybe he literally went for a swim. It doesn't matter what he did. He received his answer from the One Mind of Spirit. The truth—the solution he was seeking—was revealed to him.

There is something to be said for this walk-away strategy, for turning away from the problem and distracting yourself. Be relaxed and calm, because repeated effort defeats itself. When we stop forcing things mentally and relax, it allows our creativity to be sparked by the Divine.

Affirm

I can always walk away and allow divine answers to come.

YOU CAN'T FORCE JOY
DECEMBER 6

Christmas card photos are a great way to share your happy little family with the world. Except, sometimes, the outtakes are a much more accurate representation of reality. One of my favorite Christmas card photos was when my kids were about six, five, and two, when they were all posing together at a park. The six- and five-year-old had big phony smiles for the camera, but the youngest had her head down on a rock wall, red-faced and crying. While hilarious, that photo was not sent out to our family and friends.

After all the kids were grown up and had moved out on their own, we got a little Jack Russell that we posed with on the beach at sunset for our Christmas card photos. It was very cold out, the wind was blowing, and our photographer was not feeling well. The dog's name was Joy. Ironically, in many of the pictures, Joy was snarling and growling, showing her angry teeth. Joy did not understand or care about the idea of a happy Christmas card photo. The beach is the place where she likes to run around and look for the best sticks. She does not want to be held or forced be still. We were taking away her joy, while simultaneously trying to force her to look joyful!

Real-life joy is always better than a manufactured photo. May your joy be utterly authentic!

Affirm

Today, I choose joy!

PEACE OF MIND, NO CHARGE
DECEMBER 7

So often the stress that we experience as human beings is made up, manufactured, and serves no purpose. That's right—feeling stress is a choice. Consider the way air travel works. Airlines are always warning that there might not be enough room in the overhead bins on board, so people might have to check their luggage. This is a manufactured fear that creates unnecessary stress. Yes, your bag could be checked, but it would be placed below you on the same plane you are on. It is nothing to worry about or feel stress over.

I once met a couple on a plane who were so concerned about choosing their seat and boarding the plane early that they paid excessive fees. I saved the money and didn't pay any extra fees. I wasn't concerned at all with when I would board the plane. Do you know where I ended up sitting? Right next to them!

When flying, everyone on the flight is going to the same place in the same airplane. Be mindful of when companies are creating problems for you to worry about to try and get you to pay for peace of mind. Peace of mind is always free. It only costs the time it takes for you to think the thought and know the Truth.

Affirm

*I travel with peace and ease, knowing my way
is made clear, and all is well.
I feel no stress, only peace.*

WHO MADE A DIFFERENCE?
DECEMBER 8

Stop for a moment and think about all the people who have made a difference in your life. I suspect there are many. Make a list, even if just mentally. Now consider, of all those people, how many have you told that they made a difference in your life? How many have you thanked? The divine purpose of humanity while we are here on earth is to do kind things for others, to be compassionate, loving, and supportive. This is how we recognize our oneness and unity.

While it is not what motivates us, it feels good to receive a moment of acknowledgment when someone thanks us for influencing their life in a positive way.

Act

Consider who you can thank for making a difference in your life. Thank them!

STAND UP
DECEMBER 9

A minister friend of mine once said, "Stand for something, but against nothing." Being for something is positive and good. Being against something means you are resisting, fighting, and opposing. It is a negative use of Spiritual Law and ends up creating more of what we don't want to experience. We know Spirit responds to our faith, positive energy, and good intentions. Are you unsure what you stand for? Think of ideas, traits, and characteristics you would associate with the Divine. Be the Presence of God in the world. Stand for something good.

Act

Stand for peace instead of protesting war.
Stand for health instead of fighting a disease.
Stand for love instead of resisting hate.
Stand for abundance instead of opposing lack.
Stand for unity instead of believing in separation.

HAPPINESS MATTERS
DECEMBER 10

Why does happiness matter? Because when you are happy, positive, and optimistic, you perform better in many areas in your life, like in intelligence, creativity, energy, business, relationships, etc. So how do we "get happy?" One way is by serving others or performing acts of kindness. It has been scientifically proven that helping others triggers the feel-good chemicals in our brain, like dopamine, serotonin, and oxytocin. It literally makes us *happy* to help other people.

This altruistic practice is an opportunity to see and experience our unity and oneness. When we are able to help others—which we almost always are—it empowers us spiritually and makes us happy.

Affirm

I am always happy to serve others with kindness.

IT STARTS WITH ONE STEP
DECEMBER 11

Fitness activity trackers are a popular way to keep track of your physical movement. For many years, it was suggested that a person should average 10,000 steps a day for health benefits and proper weight management. It turns out that the 10,000 per day target number was made up and arbitrary. It was a marketing gimmick, not studied or based in science. When doctors and health experts did finally study walking steps, the actual recommended amount for optimal health was discovered to be far less, somewhere between 5,000 - 7,000 steps a day.

I think the takeaway is that forward movement is forward movement. This is true with everything, from our exercise routines to our faith and our spiritual practice. It is true for any positive change we wish to undertake in life. Your call to action is to make the effort toward your goal in whatever way feels right, however much you can. Take a step in the right direction today.

Affirm

*Today, I am committed to moving toward
the manifestation of all my desires.*

IT ISN'T REAL
DECEMBER 12

When we are young, we believe in childish things that aren't true, like monsters under the bed and scary beings in the dark. As we grow up, we start to realize that these things aren't real. We understand that we can choose what we believe in, and we don't have to believe in things that cause us pain and fear. We don't have to give power to our fears. We can, instead, give power to the Truth.

As spiritually aware adults, we can still occasionally deal with believing in scary things that aren't true. We are human, after all. But that doesn't mean we have to resign ourselves to being possessed by our proverbial demons just because we're human. Our power lies in our ability to choose our focus. We can focus on our negative thoughts and beliefs, our limitations, our fears—giving power to them like the boogeyman under the bed that once terrified us—or we can stay focused on who we are as children of God, perfect, whole, and complete.

Affirm

Today, I stand firm in my choice to believe in the good.
God is my good, and God is here now.
There is nothing to fear.

HEALTH AND WHOLENESS
DECEMBER 13

If we wish to demonstrate health for ourselves, we must embody the idea of health. While health includes our physical body, it also encompasses so much more. Health includes aspects of life that contribute to our wholeness, including freedom from disease, vigor, vitality, fitness, stamina, happiness, energy, mental wellness, economic health, emotional well-being, balance, etc. Focus today on all aspects of your health and wholeness.

Ask

What does it mean to be healthy and whole?
What does it feel like in my mind, body, and spirit?
How do I look and act when I am expressing life in healthy ways?
How do I acknowledge my emotional health?
What might need addressing in my spiritual health?
Do I feel financially healthy at this time in my life?
Is there some habit or activity that needs
releasing for the revelation of my health?
How can I best embody health and wholeness today?

BRICK BY BRICK
DECEMBER 14

Bricklayers work hard in masonry, laying bricks all day to build walls. It is tough work that takes years of training, physical strength, and great precision. Imagine if, after working all day, the bricklayer systematically knocked all the bricks down. That one act would nullify all the hard work that was done. No wall would be created. That would be silly. No bricklayer would intentionally knock down all their hard work.

Remember, the same is true for our prayer life. If you are praying, setting intentions, affirming, and expecting your good, make sure you aren't knocking it all down afterward with negative thinking, complaining, and focusing on doubt. It is like knocking down your prayers, nullifying your hard work. It takes ongoing commitment to receive your desired outcome.

Ask

*If I am not seeing the results I wish to see,
am I knocking down my work?*

THE PATH TO PEACE
DECEMBER 15

Peace belongs to everyone.
Before you are a citizen of any country, you are human.
Before you are a race or gender, you are human.
Before you are Christian, Jewish, Muslim, or any other religion, you are human.

Before you are human, you are life—a perfect soul.
Each one of us, all of us, share the experience of expressing as the Divine.
We share in the expansion of our individualized, eternal souls.
We are One Life in God, one with God—
Not just the God of our understanding,
But the God we may never understand.

Step away from labels and ideologies.
Release the belief in separation.
See the Truth.
For the good of humanity.
For the highest good of your soul.
Recognize Peace as your true divine nature.

Affirm

Peace belongs to everyone.

WHO IS THE ENEMY?
DECEMBER 16

Some churches teach of a great enemy—Satan, a devil, a sense of evil, an opposite to God that is out to challenge us, test us, or hurt us. New Thought teaches that nothing can oppose God, and nothing can separate us from God. But humans love to believe in enemies. Do you believe you have an enemy in your life?

The enemy is not another human being. It is not the government. It is not nature. New Thought philosophy teaches that the Spirit of God is within; it turns out, whatever we consider to be an enemy is also internal. The real enemy is negative thoughts, limiting beliefs, and states of low consciousness. We have the free will to believe all kinds of fearful things if we choose. The only thing that stops this cycle is our willingness to choose differently.

Ask

What if my only enemy is my own bad state of mind?
What if I no longer entertain this state of mind?

THERE ARE NO COINCIDENCES
DECEMBER 17

The God-presence is always at work in our lives, guiding and directing us. Once, while serving as an interim minister for a church, I struggled to write an upcoming sermon. Unexpectedly, I got a Facebook message with a friend request. It was a pastor I had known twenty years earlier whom I adored. I had not heard from him in over ten years.

We messaged each other and got caught up. He did not know I had worked as the director of Christian education at his former church, nor did he know I was now an ordained minister. I did not know he had retired and worked guest preaching at churches like I did. He recommended a book he had just finished reading—a story about a woman who had a near-death experience. It was written from a spiritual perspective, about her relationship with God, fully exploring her soul's purpose. The book, which I later couldn't put down, happened to be about the exact scripture I had chosen as the lectionary for that week's sermon. Out of the entire Bible, what were the odds of that? The woman's story became the basis of my sermon.

How did this old pastor and I manage to reconnect at that exact moment in time? How did that book come to end up in my hands that week? How did God know I needed help and reassurance that I was on the right path? The truth is, I don't know! I do know that the more open we are to God's Omnipresence, the more demonstrations of it we see.

Affirm

I choose to view serendipitous coincidences as divine guidance.

CHILDLIKE EXPECTATIONS
DECEMBER 18

There is a scene at the end of the 1994 version of the classic movie *Miracle on 34th Street*, after the young girl Susan has helped free her friend, Kris Kringle (Santa Claus), from jail. She receives the presents she asked him for. She gets a dad, because her mother has unexpectedly gotten married overnight. On the way to the house in the country that Susan had also asked him for, her mother insists they are going there for her work, not because the house is theirs. Susan rolls her eyes and insists, "I'm sorry, mother, but you have it perfectly wrong!" She fully expects the outcome she wishes to see, and sure enough, it is revealed in the scenes that follow that the house is theirs.

Jesus taught that we are to become like children to "enter the kingdom." We are to have an open heart full of childlike belief, trusting fully in the Power of God to manifest any outcome we desire. Oh, how hard it is for adults to do this! Expecting great things to happen is not a sign of delusion. It is a sign of great faith. When we use our word to declare our expectation of what we desire, we are using our faith. Spiritual Law responds.

Ask

Am I expecting all the great things I desire?

THINK PREPOSITIONS
DECEMBER 19

Do you remember learning about parts of speech, like prepositions, in school? Most of us don't!

Here's a quick refresher: A preposition is a word that shows the relationship between a noun or a pronoun to another word in a sentence. Think of it as a linking word or bridge word that connects two things, often expressing a relationship of place, time, or direction. Prepositions can serve a spiritual purpose, too. They are a beautiful way to understand the Omnipresence of God.

We know God is omnipresent, everywhere at all times, widespread, and constantly encountered. But to *feel* this Truth, God's Omnipresence must be understood in relation to each one of us, individually. So, how do we do that? By thinking in terms of prepositions! Many of these words paint a vivid picture of the infinite, expansive nature of Spirit in relation to our human experience.

Consider the following prepositions as descriptions of where the Divine is in relation to you. Read each one as a complete sentence: "God is ____ me."

about, above, after, along, amid, among, around, as, at, before, behind, below, beneath, beside, beyond, by, following, in, inside, near, of, on, outside, over, past, round, through, to, toward, under, upon, via, with, within

Affirm

God is always in relation to me. I am completely surrounded, fully supported, and unconditionally loved.

PERMISSION TO RETREAT
DECEMBER 20

The days leading up to the winter solstice can feel dark and gloomy. They are the days with the shortest amount of light in the northern hemisphere. Many of us just want to retreat into our homes and stay warm under the covers, and there is a reason for that. These "dark days" are just before several hopeful, religious holidays that celebrate the light. We are supposed to retreat—to go within and recognize that the light we seek is within ourselves.

No matter what spiritual tradition we follow, it is still the Light of God that we seek and ultimately find within. As the winter solstice approaches, remember, the light isn't just coming—it is already here. You are the Light. You embody the Light. Deeply consider this idea and meditate on it.

Affirm

It is safe to go within and remember I am the Light of God.

TRUST IN THE LIGHT
DECEMBER 21

The winter solstice is the one twenty-four-hour period of the year when we experience the most darkness and the least amount of light. Most parts of the United States don't even notice this because they are still experiencing between 8-9 hours of daylight. Other places in the world experience less than one hour of daylight, which would be very noticeable. People who live in darkness really appreciate the solstice because it is a promise of light to come. Every day after, there will be a little more light than before. It is guaranteed. It is a natural, scientific thing that can be calculated.

The solstice is not just a hopeful thing; it is a certainty. It is fascinating that so many faith traditions and religions celebrate holidays around this planetary event that is equated with the sun having victory over darkness and the bold assurance and expectation of light coming into the world. Whatever our faith tradition or religion, we can trust in our faith with the same level of certainty.

Affirm

I trust in the light!

SEASON OF PEACE
DECEMBER 22

The holiday season can feel hectic and chaotic, filled with parties, gatherings, shopping, gift wrapping, overcommitment, unexpected emotions, and unmet expectations. Chaos does not feel good in our bodies. Let this serve as a reminder that the organized, Infinite Intelligence of the Divine cannot be chaotic. It can only be peaceful. It expresses as peace.

If we are feeling anxious, stressed out, tense, or frazzled, it means we are not living in alignment with God. Take a moment (or even better, several moments) to remember the Divine Truth that peace is within you. Do whatever spiritual practice reminds you of this Truth. At any moment, you can make the choice to be still, go within, and breathe. Let yourself be an expression of God's Peace. Allow yourself some stillness. Let the holy sacredness of the season begin with your awareness of it. Let peace begin with *you*.

Affirm

Today, I remember that this is a season of peace.

MORE HOLIDAYS. MORE LOVE
DECEMBER 23

When my friend's children were young, she was divorced from their father. Many divorced parents have experienced the complicated challenges of sharing holidays, swapping children back and forth between Christmas Eve and Christmas Day. It never feels like anyone gets enough time to properly celebrate the holiday.

What my friend did in her family was create another holiday on December 23rd. The kids helped name it. Christmas Day was on the 25th; Christmas Eve was on the 24th. On the 23rd, the children decided it would be called Christmas Adam (because if the 24th is Christmas Eve, then the 23rd must be Christmas Adam, like Adam and Eve).

My friend is now close to eighty years old. Her children are all adults in their fifties. They still refer to December 23rd as Christmas Adam and discuss as a family how they will be celebrating Christmas Adam. This is a lovely, magical story for the 21st century. It is all about love.

Happy Christmas Adam!

Affirm

There is always enough love.

START WHERE YOU ARE
DECEMBER 24

Like Jesus in the manger, we are all given the opportunity to start where we are—even if we are in a very low place. It doesn't get much lower than being born in a stable and put in a manger—a feeding trough for farm animals. Yet, Jesus accomplished the unimaginable, growing in consciousness from that lowly place, fully awakening to his oneness and unity with God, all the way to overcoming death by demonstrating resurrection. We, too, are given the chance to rise and grow into our own Christ Consciousness. Start where you are. Make the most of your opportunity to understand your divine nature and live fully in alignment with the God-Source.

Affirm

*Starting right where I am,
I awaken to the Christ Consciousness within me.*

THE BEST GIFT
DECEMBER 25

How do you react to the gift of Christ Consciousness? There is nothing to put a bow on or unwrap. You have to go there in your mind and think about it. How do you respond to the perfect principle that Jesus taught and demonstrated for all humanity? What do you do with a gift like this?

We have to commit to receiving the gift, and it is easier than you might think. Are you aware of your own Christ Consciousness—the One Presence of God within you that sparks and animates your being? We receive this gift simply by acknowledging it with our awareness.

The next thing to do with this gift is to use it. We do this by always recognizing and knowing our true nature and our true wholeness, like Jesus did. This is no small task, but it's the best part of getting such a great gift. It is our choice to do the spiritual work to remain open to the possibility of a higher consciousness every day. This is the key to awakening and living our highest, best lives.

Merry Christmas!

Affirm

I commit to receiving the gift of Christ Consciousness.
I recognize my true nature.

IT'S ALL GOD
DECEMBER 26

Life is. I am.
This side. That side.
In the seed. Through the tree.
As the fruit.
In you. In me.
Life is. God is.
I Am that I Am.
All that I see,
Life, reflected back at me.
God of my heart.
God in the sky.
All One. All God.
Embrace it. Love it. Breathe it.
Spend it. Save it. Use it.
Hold it tight. Let it go.
Life returns.
It never left. It always is.
I am this. I am that.
I am. Life is.

Affirm

I am Life expressing as me.

"I DO..."
DECEMBER 27

Most people at some point in their lives have attended a wedding ceremony. Vows and promises are made before family and friends, and the entire public moment is considered sacred, binding, and celebratory. The couple declares their love, support, and commitment to one another. They often say things like, "I promise to love, honor, and cherish you," or "I vow to stand by you no matter what challenges we face," or "I choose you for the rest of my life."

Have you ever considered making such statements to yourself? It sounds silly, but what if we took a moment to commit to loving ourselves in the same way we commit to supporting our spouse? You are a very important person in your life. You have been with yourself for your entire life, and you will be with yourself until the day you make your transition back to the spiritual realm. Take this moment to shift your attention to loving yourself. Make this vow to yourself.

Act

_____ *(your name), we have been through a lot together, and there is no one else I would want to spend my life with. In this moment of deep awareness, I choose and promise to love, honor, and cherish you every day of my life. This includes consciously and lovingly supporting you in mind, body, and spirit. I intend to encourage your dreams, remind you of healthy choices, suggest self-care, and know the Truth of your divine spiritual perfection. It is my great joy in life to love you as much as God loves you. No matter what challenges we might face, I have your back. I commit to loving you, fully, forever.*

THANK YOU TRIGGERS
DECEMBER 28

Making a gratitude list can get old fast, but gratitude as a spiritual practice need not be boring. Instead of a list, consider shifting your way of thinking to a state of appreciation. Daily experiences can trigger you to do this. Here are some examples:

- You find something expired in the back of the refrigerator. That is a trigger to be grateful for your abundance of good food.
- You turn on your kitchen faucet or bathtub. What a great reminder to be grateful for clean, running water.
- You hear an ambulance go down the street. That is an opportunity to be grateful for your good health and that doctors and hospitals exist.
- You hear your heater click on. What a wonderful reminder to be thankful for your cozy, warm home.
- You get a text from a friend. Stop and be grateful because that person is in your life.
- Your alarm goes off for work. What an opportunity to accept your prosperity and abundance.

All day long, we experience things that can trigger the awareness of our gratitude—if we choose to see it that way. Being in a state of appreciation puts us more in vibrational alignment with God's good, which is our good.

Affirm

I am grateful for all the ways I experience my good.

PICTURE IT...
DECEMBER 29

The coming new year is a blank slate filled with opportunity, and it is a wonderful time to create a vision board. Think about what you want to draw into your life experience. Envision it, dream it, and display it in a way that inspires you.

Always remember to include world peace on your vision board. While the idea sounds cliché, we will never have peace if we aren't individually including world peace in our desires, intentions, and visualizations. What would it look like and feel like if our world was a peaceful place? Perhaps this is the year it happens because so many awakened souls are envisioning it. Three words to keep in mind when creating a vision board are: *have*, *do*, and *be*.

Ask

What do I want to have?
Yes, material possessions are fun to think about!
There is nothing wrong with this.

What do I want to do?
Think activities and experiences.
This is where you set your goals.
What, who, and how do I want to be?
How do I want to see myself in the coming year?

What do I look like?
Who am I in relation to the world?
How do I want to feel?
How do I think Spirit sees me?

THANKS FOR THE MEMORIES
DECEMBER 30

At the end of December, many of us wonder where the year has gone. What did we even do all year? How quickly we forget! A fun exercise to jog your memory is to use the photo storage app on your phone. Spend a few minutes going through all the photos you took during the past year. You took photos of people you loved, things you thought were beautiful, events you enjoyed attending, and things worth capturing and celebrating. It's amazing how we rarely take the time to go back through the photos we take.

Scrolling through the past year of photos is a way to see the many demonstrations of your good. It helps you end the year in a state of gratitude, remembering and appreciating good times. You will be surprised to see how much good you experienced! This is a pleasant way to wrap up the current year and release it gratefully. What will you take photos of next year?

Affirm

I deeply appreciate my good.
I celebrate and give thanks for my spiritual awareness.
I am grateful.

AMEN
DECEMBER 31

Amen is a declaration, an affirmation. It expresses agreement and is often said to conclude a prayer. *Amen* can mean: "so be it," "hearty approval," and "solemn ratification." Common English translations of *amen* also include: "Verily," "it is true," and "let it be so."

And So It Is has a similar meaning. When you complete an Affirmative Prayer or Spiritual Mind Treatment, and you have the realization that within your consciousness is what you are praying for, you declare: "And So It Is." The non-spiritual meaning of *And So It Is*, ironically, is "something happened as someone predicted it would." It is said after the demonstration takes place.

Using language like this after prayers dates back centuries, with another variation being the archaic: "So mote it be," or "So may it be," to affirm the prayer's wish for it to come true.

This is the conclusion of a book that contains prayers, meditations, deep questioning, stories, and reminders for how to live in alignment with Source, especially during uncertain, challenging times. While this is the last entry of daily guidance, it is my sincere hope that you continue to apply the wisdom of spiritual principles and live your best life each day.

Affirm

*I am strong and confident in my faith.
I recognize my unity with the Divine
and welcome a wonderful life experience.
I am grateful.*

And So It Is. Amen.

INDEX

A

Abundance
Jan 7, Jan 9, Mar 2, Mar 10, Apr 23, May 17, Jun 10, Jun 30, Aug 16, Sep 20, Oct 8, Nov 10

Affirmations
Jan 10, Jan 21, Mar 7, Mar 19, Apr 18, May 19, Jul 5, Nov 9

Awakening
Jan 27, Mar 3, Mar 14, July 6, July 22, Aug 25, Sept 27

Awareness
Jan 16, Mar 12, Aug 21, Aug 25, Sep 8, Sep 22, Oct 24, Nov 4, Dec 25

B

Balance
Feb 29, Nov 23

Beauty
Jul 11, Jul 20, Sep 30, Oct 28

Beliefs
Apr 13, Apr 19, Apr 30, May 18, May 23, Jun 21, Jun 22, Jul 15, Aug 26, Dec 12

Breathing
Feb 18, Mar 29, Aug 3

C

Consciousness
Feb 20, Apr 4, Apr 21, Jun 9, Jul 13, Aug 5, Sep 11, Nov 16, Dec 24

Creative Process
Mar 20, Dec 14

Creativity (Work)
Feb 25, Mar 13, Apr 11, Nov 25, Dec 5

D

Divinity (Divine Nature)
Jan 15, Jan 17, Jan 20, Jan 22, Jan 24, Feb 1, Feb 17, Feb 20, Mar 5, Mar 30, Apr 2, May 2, May 6, May 8, Jul 19, Aug 27, Oct 3, Oct 18, Nov 12

E

Eternal Life
Apr 8, Apr 29, Jun 13, Jun 24, Aug 12, Aug 18, Oct 31, Dec 4

F

Faith
Jan 8, Jan 18, Mar 17, April 1, Apr 15, May 11, Jun 2, Nov 11, Nov 27, Dec 18

Fear/Worry
Jan 29, Feb 22, July 27, Aug 13, Sep 18, Nov 17

Forgiveness
Feb 4, Mar 23, Aug 22, Sep 28

G

Good (Be the Good, Focus on the Good, See the Good)
Sep 16, Oct 26, Oct 28, Nov 2, Nov 20

Gratitude
Jan 11, Feb 22, Mar 16, Apr 22, Sep 9, Oct 8, Oct 11, Oct 19, Nov 24, Dec 28, Dec 30

Guidance
Feb 25, Mar 4, Apr 10, Jun 7, Jun 14, Oct 27, Dec 17

H

Health/Healing
Jan 10, Feb 12, Feb 16, Feb 22, Mar 22, Apr 5, May 31, Jul 1, Jul 31, Aug 10, Sep 9, Sep 28, Oct 4, Oct 30, Nov 6, Dec 13

I

I AM
Mar 19, May 2, Aug 6

Imagination
Jan 2, Feb 9, Mar 31, Sep 17, Sep 26, Oct 21

Interfaith
Jan 13, Jan 26, Mar 8, Jun 3, Jul 8, Nov 15

J-K

Joy
Jan 23, Feb 15, Apr 26, Aug 31, Sep 15, Nov 1, Dec 6

L

Law of Attraction
Mar 9, Jun 11, Jun 20, Sep 21

Light
Sep 24, Dec 1, Dec 20, Dec 21

Love
Feb 14, May 20, Jun 26, Jul 12, Sep 19

M-N

Meditation (about meditation)
Feb 18, Jun 6, Sep 14

Meditations
May 7, May 20, Jun 18, Jul 29

Miracles
Jan 24, May 26, Oct 12

O

Omnipresence
Jan 31, Mar 15 , May 10, Dec 19

Oneness
Jan 5, Feb 5, Mar 18, Oct 1, Nov 7, Nov 15, Nov 29

P-Q

Peace
Jan 19, Jan 25, Jan 28, Feb 23, Feb 28, Apr 27, Jun 23, Jul 9, Oct 25, Nov 21, Dec 7, Dec 15, Dec 22

Perfection
Apr 6, Jun 28, Jul 15, Aug 17, Sep 10

Possibility
Jan 1, Jan 28, Mar 31, Apr 17, Jun 21, Aug 4, Oct 23

Prayer (about prayer)
Feb 10, Feb 11, Feb 12, Feb 13, Mar 28, Apr 28, Jul 21, Aug 14, Dec 31

Prayers (for various topics)
Jan 25, Feb 12, Feb 16, Apr 9, Apr 11, Apr 27, May 24, Jul 4, Jul 12, Jul 23, Aug 23, Sep 13, Oct 16

Present Moment
Jan 16, Jul 18, Jul 24, Sep 4

R

Relationships
Feb 4, Feb 5, Apr 21, Sep 28, Oct 14, Nov 6, Dec 8

S

Self-Care/Self Love
Aug 20, Sep 3, Sep 5, Dec 2, Dec 27

Sin
Jan 15, Jun 27, Jul 25

Spiritual Practice
Mar 24, Apr 7, Apr 25, Jun 8, June 17, Nov 13

Stillness
Feb 2, Feb 18, Apr 14, Jun 4, Jul 17, Aug 15, Sep 25, Oct 5, Dec 22

T-U

Thoughts
Jan 12, Jan 20, Mar 26, Apr 3, Apr 12, May 1, May 13, May 23, Jun 12, Jun 22, Jul 28, Aug 1, Aug 28, Sep 6, Oct 2, Nov 3, Nov 14

Transformation
May 9, May 12, Jul 6, Jul 26, Oct 29

Trust
Jan 4, Feb 24, Aug 11, Dec 5

Truth
Jan 6, Aug 26, Nov 19

V

Vibration (Energy, Frequency)
Jan 30, Feb 15, Apr 14

Visualization
Jan 2, May 25, Oct 6, Dec 29

W-X-Y-Z

Word (Power of our word)
Jan 14, Feb 21, Jul 3, Sep 12

ACKNOWLEDGMENTS

I could not have written this book without the love and support of various family members, teachers, editors, spiritual centers, and schools. I live in a deep state of gratitude.

Thank you to my husband, Gary, for chauffeuring me to speaking engagements, showing up every time I am convinced I need an extra audience member, and unwittingly steering me toward the title of this book. (He is right; all we ever need is something good to think about!) Thank you for letting me systematically read one rough-draft entry to you every single night back in 2025. You helped this book come alive. I love you.

Thank you to my children, bonus children, and grandchildren, especially the ones who trust me with their spiritual questions, manifestation desires, and prayer requests. I love you all and will continue to know the highest good for your lives. A special thank you to my stepdaughter, Melissa Paulsen, who edited the heck out of this book.

Thank you to Stacey Smekofske, of Edits by Stacey, LLC, for making me sound way more professional than I really am and for finding all those extra spaces at the end of about a thousand paragraphs. Sorry about that!

I have a unique team of spiritual friends who not only uplift, inspire, and encourage me, but also hold me accountable when I get off track. They are all lightworkers in their own way. To say I appreciate their support is an understatement. I thank Trina Gheen, Julie Yoast, and all the gals at Universal Heart Center in Crescent City, CA.

Thank you to my friends at Unity of Bandon, and to their Senior Minister, Rev. Robin Haruna. You all make me a better speaker, teacher, author, and I'm glad to know every single one of you.

Thank you to CSL Midtown, Atlanta, for always cheering me on to my next endeavor, including my incredible prayer partners, Mya Fuller, RScP and Judy Aehle, RScP.

A big thank you to Emerson Theological Institute for accepting the rough draft of this manuscript as the required project for the completion of my Doctorate of Divinity. I am still in awe of how delightful the whole process was, and I'm grateful for the teachers and administrators I met there, including Rev. Dr. John Karn, Rev. Dr. Melissa Higginbotham, and Provost Rev. Dr. Ruth Miller.

I still believe I had the best parents a girl could ever ask for. Thank you, Carol and Raymond Wickes, for bringing me into this world and then, after your transitions, showing me there is so much more to it than this earthly life.

Always and forever, I thank God, Spirit, Universe, Source, for expressing in me, through me, and as me. This book is full of God's ideas, and I'm fortunate to be able to put my name on it. I am grateful.

ABOUT THE AUTHOR

Rev. Dr. Cynthia Paulsen is a New Thought minister, licensed Divine Science Practitioner, motivational speaker, and author known for making spiritual principles practical, inclusive, and transformative. She holds a Doctorate of Divinity and a Master's degree in Holistic Theology, with extensive training in The Science of Mind®, metaphysics, affirmative prayer, and spiritual healing. Her teachings are heartfelt, accessible, and grounded in both wisdom and lived experience. Through her sermons, workshops, and private practice, she guides others in cultivating inner peace, deep healing, and a conscious connection with the Divine.

ALSO BY CYNTHIA PAULSEN

Undoing the Knots

Reclaiming Our Good

Made in the USA
Coppell, TX
06 March 2026